ADVANCE PRAISE FOR

Examining Images of Urban Life:
A Resource for Teachers of Young Adult Literature

"From Baltimore to New Orleans, from El Paso to LA, *Examining Images of Urban Life: A Resource for Teachers of Young Adult Literature* analyzes young adult stories from 'uptown, midtown, downtown, up the hill, down the hill, along the river,' and various urban ethnic enclaves. This book disputes formulaic portrayals of urban youth, balancing as the editors explain, 'the gritty with the edifying.' The Drs. Nicosia have assembled an all-star cast of authors and scholars to reconsider the stereotypical portrayal of the so-called 'urban core,' thoroughly analyzing urban characters, conflict, and context in young adult literature. A must- have for every middle and high school English language arts teacher."

Dr. James Blasingame
Professor of Young Adult Literature
Arizona State University
Executive Director of the Assembly on Literature for Adolescents
of the National Council of Teachers of English

"This terrific and timely collection gives cities their due—not as dark and 'gritty' places but as challenging, rich, exciting environments in which people can grow and thrive. While affirming the urban, the book also cautions against the dismissal of suburban and rural life; the general takeaway is that human communities are complex and should be respected. I love the mix of creative and critical voices. Anyone working with young people and YA literature will find this book moving as well as instructive."

Dr. Kenneth Kidd, Professor of English, University of Florida
Forthcoming book: *Theory for Beginners: Children's Literature as Critical Thought*, Fordham University Press

"Beginning with the introduction, it is clear that Laura and James have pulled together a collection of chapters that celebrate the modern city as presented in Young Adult Literature. The various authors not only examine complex presentations of images within urban settings; they reveal how adolescents find themselves and a community among the teeming streets they inhabit. For those of us who teach in diverse schools and universities in large cities this volume is an essential addition to our reference materials."

Dr. Steven T. Bickmore
Associate Professor of English Education University of Nevada, Las Vegas
Past President of the Assembly on Literature for Adolescents of NCTE

"Gatsby, Gossip Girls, gentrification, genre. These are just a few of the focal points through which young adult literature is viewed in this remarkable collection of essays about the images of urban life in contemporary and classic literature. This is not simply an examination of setting. It is, instead, the difference Richard Peck points out when he includes, 'Why is the story set where it is?' in his questions to ask about a YA novel. Thinking about the purpose of the where and the when of setting provides the need for a more critical eye in literary analysis. Nicosia and Nicosia gather voices from academia to explore not only important titles by Older and Reynolds, Williams-Garcia, and others but to suggest questions to extend beyond the text."

Dr. Teri Lesesne, Distinguished Professor of Library science
Sam Houston State University, Texas

"*Examining Images in Urban Life: A Resource for Teachers of Young Adult Literature* features important voices on young adult literature in urban settings. Essays from award-winning YA authors like Benjamin Alire Saenz enhance critical perspectives from scholars of contemporary reads found on today's bestseller lists. This is a valuable addition to current conversations about the most popular category of fiction, and will be of particular interest to those teaching children's and young adult literature courses in colleges and universities, as well as those training preservice high school English teachers."

Dr. Ebony Elizabeth Thomas, Associate Professor, University of Pennsylvania
and author of *The Dark Fantastic: Race and the Imagination from Harry Potter to The Hunger Games.*

"Laura and James Nicosia offer a necessary and compelling resource to educators with their latest collection *Examining Images of Urban Life: A Resource for Teachers of Young Adult Literature.* Recognizing a need in classrooms to move beyond so-called canonical classics that simply cannot offer contemporary youth an abundant cache of literature that acknowledges racial and cultural diversity; differential gender orientations; recent sites of conflict and complexity; let alone the recent 'abundance of sociological, psychological, political, educational, and reference' texts that acknowledge the complexity of life in urban settings; the Nicosias' collection broadens the current scope of the city as a site of consideration for educators and young adults alike. The contributors offer a panoply of discussions from a myriad manner of perspectives. Award-winning authors such as Benjamin Alire Sáenz are couched between eighth-grade instructors such as Katie Slutier and Cambridge University faculty like Karen Coats providing one of the greatest strengths in the anthology: the differentiated perceptions and overlapping discourse communities found between two covers. This volume will greatly inform and expand the instructor's base of scholarship and perspective on known YA/ChL work while easily offering them brave new works and perspectives of the city, its inhabitants, and the possibilities contained within."

Dr. Joseph Michael Sommers, Professor of English, Central Michigan University,
editor of three books on Neil Gaiman including his most recent:
Conversations With Neil Gaiman (2018).

EXAMINING IMAGES OF URBAN LIFE

Copyright © 2021 | Myers Education Press, LLC

Published by Myers Education Press, LLC
P.O. Box 424
Gorham, ME 04038

All rights reserved. No part of this book may be reprinted or reproduced in any form or by any electronic, mechanical, or other means, now known or hereafter invented, including photocopying, recording, and information storage and retrieval, without permission in writing from the publisher.

Myers Education Press is an academic publisher specializing in books, e-books, and digital content in the field of education. All of our books are subjected to a rigorous peer review process and produced in compliance with the standards of the Council on Library and Information Resources.

LIBRARY OF CONGRESS CATALOGING-IN-PUBLICATION DATA AVAILABLE FROM LIBRARY OF CONGRESS
13-digit ISBN 978-1-9755-0244-7 (paperback)
13-digit ISBN 978-1-9755-0243-0 (hardcover)
13-digit ISBN 978-1-9755-0245-4 (library networkable e-edition)
13-digit ISBN 978-1-9755-0246-1 (consumer e-edition)

Printed in the United States of America

All first editions printed on acid-free paper that meets the American National Standards Institute Z39-48 standard.

Books published by Myers Education Press may be purchased at special quantity discount rates for groups, workshops, training organizations, and classroom usage. Please call our customer service department at 1-800-232-0223 for details.

Cover design by Teresa Lagrange.

Visit us on the web at **www.myersedpress.com** to browse our complete list of titles.

EXAMINING IMAGES OF URBAN LIFE

A Resource for Teachers of Young Adult Literature

EDITED BY LAURA M. NICOSIA
AND JAMES F. NICOSIA

Gorham, Maine

Table of Contents

INTRODUCTION

Celebrating the City

Laura M. Nicosia and James F. Nicosia

Our desire to map the city is a desire to map the self.

—MARIA BEVILLE (2019, 1)

BOTH OF US were born and raised in large cities in northern New Jersey. Each of us grew up in attached shotgun row houses in an immediate neighborhood that housed dozens of varied immigrant and first-generation American families. We walked to our local elementary schools, walked to the corner parks where we played with any number of several dozen kids our age, and walked to the local family-owned delis where we shopped for most of our groceries. Summers smelled of Noxzema, Sea & Ski suntan lotion, and Mr. Softee ice cream on the front stoop while our moms sat in folding chairs and talked about Vietnam and the weekly Casey Kasem countdown. Community building was as easy as serving a pitcher of iced coffee to the moms and offering a do-it-yourself project to the dads or a cherry freeze pop to the kids. Summers in the city were sensual extravaganzas of noise and heat, complaint, and celebration, and open fire hydrants.

We referred to the various sections of town as uptown, midtown, downtown, up the hill, down the hill, along the river, the Ironbound, and so forth. There was an Italian section, a German section, a Jewish section, an Arabic section, and a Spanish section of town. Each neighborhood had its own flavors, its own scents, its own sounds. They were cities-within-cities. When we were old enough, we might take the bus to visit high school friends and walk the main shopping drag of "Downtown" or "City Center," but most of what we needed was within a ten-block radius. Our places of play, our places to shop, our friends, and our lives revolved around our immediate neighborhoods. We had every kind of foodstuff imaginable within walking distance, including two fish shops and a live chicken market.

The gridded streets were often one-way, so even car traffic was well diffused, ensuring that the flow of activity within the city was distributed equally; indeed, in the modern city, activity may be found everywhere. The few scattered dead-end streets were hotbeds for activity in another way: children funneled into them to partake in street games (manhunt, stickball, double Dutch, May I, Would You Rather, I Dare You To, Simon Sez, and Red Light/Green Light), but expediency often meant playing right there, in the street, in front of your home. The utterance "car" meant one thing to kids in this context: you had to temporarily halt your game and empty the street because one was coming.

We paint a nostalgic picture, perhaps, but make no mistake. Growing up in the city was not all Norman Rockwell and idyllic playtime. There were drugs and alcohol. There were gangs. There was La Cosa Nostra. We had little open space and no lawns. Privacy was a rare privilege. Neighbors who shared common walls heard all but the quietest conversations. But we also were serenaded by practicing vocal groups as infants: Dion and the Belmonts were named after the street, Belmont Avenue, beyond the backyard. For each disturbing element, there was a reassuring one; for each warning, there was a celebration.

In an increasingly dualistic society, American attitudes tend to pair off rural with bucolic, urban with gritty, the pastoral with the good, the city with the bad. This is an oversimplification for America's past; it is oversimplification today. Writers know this. People who live in cities know this. Yet the facile portrayal of cities in popular culture exemplifies one-note or one-story elements of the cities, something that cities exactly are not. Urban spaces are dynamic places, variegated from neighborhood to neighborhood, block to block, building to building, house to house, apartment to apartment. Yet it has become too easy to create yet another "hard-hitting, gritty drama of gang violence on the basketball court." Real cities continue to defy such oversimplification. And the writers that are celebrated in this work are applauded here for their sensitivity to the dynamic place that is the American city.

Why We Compiled This Book

> *As the geographic, cultural, and economic distinctions of cities are taken for granted, there are even broader implications for readers, teachers, and critics of adolescent literature.*
>
> —EBONY ELIZABETH THOMAS (2011, 13)

We teach English at Montclair State University, a large public institution of higher education, in northern New Jersey with nearly 20,000 students. Our university has been named a Hispanic-serving institution by the U.S. Department of Education to recognize our "unprecedented growth and . . . commitment to providing underserved populations access to affordable higher education" (Montclair State University n.d.). The students in our classes, for a large part, *come* from the urban feeding districts of the tri-state area (New York, New Jersey, Pennsylvania), and our teacher certification candidates are sent to more than 21 districts across our state—many settings of which are urban.

We see what students in public high schools read across New Jersey, and many of those texts paint a troubled and negative portrait of living in a city (gangs, crime, violence, drugs, pollution, looting, and so on). Although these elements of urban living are present in many cities across the United States, there is so much more to acknowledge and on which we can focus our thoughts and balance the gritty with the edifying.

Through our work in the schools, we see a surge in not only the presence of contemporary young adult literature (YAL) in reading lists—but also the presence of outdated texts that (perhaps) do not speak to the students who are holding those books in their hands during class. *The Outsiders* (S.E. Hinton 1967) is a fine novel with applicable lessons, perhaps, for today's classroom, but the 1967 novel is of and from a time before most of our students' *parents'* era! Surely there are other portrayals of the city that are more immediately recognizable to the young people of the twenty-first century that can augment our classrooms. We all want our youths to see themselves in the texts they read, and our collection suggests texts that speak to a more full urban experience with an open mind and offers new ways of looking at books that teachers may already be using in their curriculum, but more likely not. Reading (or rereading) urban fiction with a new perspective may dispel the media-driven, anecdotally propagated preconceptions about city living. Any number of these essays can serve as a resource in urban settings, wherein teachers can select books that mirror and advocate for the very students sitting in their classes.

Despite the abundance of sociological, psychological, political, educational, and reference books on life in urban settings, there are no collections exclusively focused on examining what it means to live in urban environments as depicted in contemporary and popular young adult literature. Although there are numerous articles in journals, trade magazines, and scholarly editions, no single book explores how life is depicted in the city in popular fiction. Consequently, educators and teachers-in-training do not have a resource to help them focus their lessons and conversations on this topic of urban cultural and geographic diversity.

This collection gathers contributions from scholars and authors who consider how living in a city affects character identity and growth, and the ways authors world-build the urban setting in dynamic and powerful ways. There are novels that portray the city as magical places; others as stifling, imposing environments; and others still that limn the city as a harsh but beautiful living landscape. Cities can be the center of culture, business, and the arts, and are the meeting places for diversities of all kinds. Urban environments are not all filled with violence, racial tensions, drugs, gangs, basketball, and homelessness—although these may be present. More important, young people need not always be limned as victims of the city. They are products of the city, themselves rich in diversity of race, culture, and opinion. The urban cityscape plays an important role in how characters relate to each other, how plots develop, and how individual youths and adolescents cultivate a sense of self.

This collection revolves around a reconsideration of what the city represents to its readers and to its inhabitants. Too often today, audiences hear the words *city* or *urban* and automatically envision one thing. A pet peeve of ours is the term so loosely bandied about that it has become a buzzword adjective for anything urban: *gritty*. Urban life is varied and rich, and its literature is both, as well. Like any other setting, it may be gritty, or it may not be. Unlike any other setting, it is dynamic, performative, and symbiotic. That is, the city defines its inhabitants (and its literary characters) at the same time as it is being defined by its inhabitants (and its literary characters). These essays attempt to initiate a discussion into a wider view of what the city is, to reconsider sociocultural and literary clichés. Readers will come away with a sense of empowerment and understanding that city dwellers are vast and empowered, not "of a type" and casualties of a harsh existence. Even when growing up in difficult conditions, twenty-first-century YAL, at its best, imbues its characters and readers with a sense of empowerment and agency.

Educators in all disciplines, at all levels, will benefit from reading this collection and from teaching it in their classrooms. The thrust of this book is not limited to instructors in the humanities, however. Rather, we aim at a broader recognition for all readers that critiques preconceived notions of cities as "scary places" where "those people" live. Teachers and readers in urban areas will find it easy to recognize the flavors, sounds, and textures of a living, exciting place to live. Those outside the urban landscape will be awakened to a new understanding that a city is not literarily synonymous with "a place where only bad things happen."

The Conceptual Framework for These Essays

> *Reading about different kinds of places may change students' previously held views about cities, or in the case of city dwellers, affirm their sense of identity and belonging. As they are transported into these urban spaces through literature, young adults expand their view of the world and what it means to be a citizen in it.*
>
> —EBONY ELIZABETH THOMAS (2011, 14)

We base much of our understanding of the term urban literature on Sandra Hughes-Hassell and Sandy L. Guild's fine 2002 essay in *The ALAN Review* where they identify nine characteristic commonalities of realistic depictions of city life in YAL:

1. The racial and ethnic makeup of the urban communities varies.
2. A broad range of socioeconomic levels is represented.
3. Perceptive authors capture the language of modern urban youth.

4. The best young adult books about urban adolescents convey a strong sense of community.
5. The dangers of inner-city life are realistically depicted.
6. One theme shared across books written about urban youth is a sense of survival, both physical and psychological.
7. Young adult novels about urban youth deal with issues of importance to all teens.
8. Celebration of family is an important feature of young adult literature about urban youth.
9. Much of the literature about urban young adults incorporates some aspect of cultural history or heritage and conveys a feeling of ethnic pride and identity. (35–39)

How to Read This Book

> *Thus, the city is where the subject and space become intertwined. While the city becomes part of the subject and the subject a part of the city, urban space in its resistance of representation remains a constant challenge to notions of self, of sameness, of homogeneity.*
>
> —MARIA BEVILLE (2019, 1)

Following each essay are pedagogically focused questions to consider, designed to offer insights into how the essays may be used as correlative readings with the primary texts. We also offer resources for further consideration and reference. These materials situate each essay, and the book as a whole, as a useful resource for the courses listed earlier and as a resource for in-service teachers who wish to expand their curricular lists.

Bookending each section of the collection are essays by noted YAL writers, e.E. Charlton-Trujillo, Benjamin Alire Sáenz (author of *Aristotle and Dante Discover the Secrets of the Universe*), Maria Andreu (author of *The Secret Side of Empty*), and Mary Rand Hess (co-author of *Solo* and *Swing*). These pieces offer the unique perspectives of the authors who place the settings of (many of) their books in cities because of the richness, textures, and complexities of urban landscapes.

Our authors' biographies and information are provided at the end of the collection, and we encourage you to seek out their scholarship for further reading. All our contributors are experts in their fields and we are proud of this gathering of sensitive, scholarly academics and educators.

The city can be anything and can contain anything; educators and community leaders should recognize the varied experiences contained therein. There is no "single story" for a city, and this is something to remember, take to heart, and celebrate. At any given moment in time, in any given city in America, everything is happening. Certainly writers throughout American literary history have created a multiplicity of city stories, and the time is ripe for sharing them with each other. We hope you find this book useful, enjoyable, enlightening, and empowering.

References

Beville, Maria. 2019. "Introduction: Otherness and the Urban." *Otherness: Essays & Studies* 7(1): 1–8. https://www.otherness.dk/journal/otherness-essays-studies-71/.

Hinton, S. E. 1967. *The Outsiders*. New York: Viking Press/Dell Publishing.

Hughes-Hassell, Sandra, and Sandy L. Guild. 2002. "The Urban Experience in Recent Young Adult Novels." *The ALAN Review* 29(3): 35–39.

Montclair State University. N.d. "Commitment to Diversity." http://www.montclair.edu.

Thomas, Ebony Elizabeth. 2011. "Landscapes of City and Self: Place and Identity in Urban Young Adult Literature." *The ALAN Review* 38(2): 13–22.

CHAPTER ONE

An Author's Perspective: Finding Your Place in the Landscape

e.E. Charlton-Trujillo

Landscape. It's the space that is around us. The sound, the rhythm, the rhyme. The assonance, the tonality, the texture. It's the putrid smell of garbage, overflowing from a two-lid dumpster. It's the man, standing in Jefferson Square, New Orleans, singing opera in the rain to his girlfriend. It's the pounding of shoes on the pavement, a horns-honking cacophony of beautiful noise music. It is the person sitting across the room, clicking their pen while watching the world extend with another launch into space.

How writers choose to utilize setting can transform the ordinary into the extraordinary. To do that, we must also remember to look beyond stereotypes—images we've seen in movies and online. Yes, there can be crime, wealth, disadvantage, but there is also strength, humanity and community among the urban landscape. It can be a place where kids might learn how to grow food and seed knowledge in a community garden. A place where families gather around a table to celebrate their days and nights. It can also be a place where thousands of people unify in protest with cardboard signs and rolling chants for justice and systemic change.

Urban can be the grit, the grind, the shove on the subway, the mumbling homeless man needing a place to rest, to eat. Brick by brick, stone by stone, a city's silhouette is owned by its people—and its visitors. As writers, we bring that into focus. Our work is our interpretation of this ever-evolving landscape of asphalt, business, and industry—of immeasurable opportunity.

Let's break down this idea of setting for a moment. We've all taken school pictures, right? Imagine sitting on the stool in front of the camera, the backdrop behind you. Maybe the backdrop is teal. Maybe it's deep purple. The photographer says, "Smile," and click/flash! Off you go. Now, imagine sitting at the same teal-maybe-purple backdrop. Then someone drops it to the floor, revealing a wall of hundreds of slithering tail-shaking rattlesnakes, coiled, tongues flapping. Some strike, slamming their heads against the glass. A siren blares. The earth shakes. A crack forms along the case, splintering up the side. The pattern of the splinter looks like a scar on your right hand. Before you can run, the case. . . .

For the record, I don't like snakes!

Also, for the record, I share this to illustrate how setting can inform story. Version one, calm, ordinary, and—eh, a bit boring. Version two, depending on your affection for reptiles, is more immediate. When stories prioritize setting, it shifts from the bland backdrop to something active and specific.

Some books sparingly describe the setting around and between their characters, kind of a less-is-more approach, and that can absolutely work. Other stories need more. Being a filmmaker as well as a writer, I often see story in camera angles. I'm always thinking about what the camera sees. What is the most specific and critical part to focus on?

Here are two examples set against an urban landscape that go from lean description to more specific.

> Standing in Chinatown, everything I knew about the world changed.

That paints an image in the mind, right (assuming you have some familiarity with some American city's Chinatown section)? Now the same concept but with more detail to the setting and character:

Chinatown.
New York City.
Two weeks before the 1st anniversary

9/11.

I'm a foreigner.
A new resident.
A hopeful, small-town, wide-eyed
Mexican American.
I am dreaming
in excited fear
to make it in the film industry—

here

It all begins
in Chinatown.
New York City.
The airport shuttle driver
sets my duffle
on the cracked sidewalk.
A tip,
a smile
and he's off.
Swerving,
merging into traffic . . .

Alone
in Chinatown.
New York City.
Surrounded by The Big Luscious Apple's
history . . .
history I learned in books/movies/TV.

Statue of Liberty.
Harlem Renaissance.

The Stonewall Riots.
Summer of Sam.
Crime in the streets.
Tactical plain clothes police.
Ball drops in Time Square.
Central Park trees—
Central Park Five wrongly accused—
Justice denied.
The Towers.
The Towers collapse . . .
and all of the world
gasped.

Overwhelmed
I pause.
Close-my-eyes pause.

Me.
Chinatown.
New York City.
Honking horns,
bus brakes exhale.
A woman plays cello on a street corner.
Birds chirping in a nest.
Basketballs dribbling,
rattling of chain link nets.
The smell of cold fish,
warm fried rice,
greasy peperoni pizza,
   spilled beer,
      chicken tacos
         exhaust fumes,
Black Jack Gum . . .

A breeze.
An ease.

Chinatown.
New York City.
Me
on a side street
with a duffle
a backpack
and a borrowed brass key.
Facing
a single red door.
A five-flight walk-up.
An apartment that isn't mine.

I'm excited-scared.
I'm excited-afraid.
I'm . . . excited for whatever comes next.

The difference is palpable. From compressed to expressed through additional detail. When discussing sensory detail or setting, we are talking about the physical space and the character's relationship to it. My first novel, *Prizefighter en Mi Casa* (Charlton-Trujillo 2007), was set in a fictional urban setting. As with all my novels, *Prizefighter en Mi Casa* addresses themes of family, friendship, racial disparities, and class. Although it could have been set in my small-town, South Texas hometown, it wouldn't have relayed the breadth of divides I wanted, the divides in physical space and emotional space. The idea of bringing the Mexican folklore I grew up with into a more urban setting.

It's the story of a Mexican American girl whose family is in peril after an accident has left her father disabled and her with severe epilepsy. Unable to work, her father reaches out to a friend and renowned Mexican prizefighter El Jefe, a man with a checkered past. Chula's *abuelita* describes him as "dark as Death." He is regarded through *chisme*, gossip, to be El Cacooey or the Mexican boogeyman.

From page one, it was important to conjure the shadowy, mythical figure against a realistic urban landscape. As if the eerie darkness of night were his own shadow:

> A gutted pumpkin glowed from across the street. The streetlight closest to the house got shot out almost one whole year ago, so I could barely see nothing. Nothing but the glowing orange head without a body. I sat on the porch swing hoping to stay outta Mama's way. She was in one of those moods again where she cursed the saints she'd be praying to later. Being Mexican and Catholic requires a lot of prayers. Even if they never seem to be answered . . . the latch on the gate banged shut only I couldn't see nothing but a shape, a moving shadow with footsteps. Footsteps that made the porch stairs cry and moan. It walked right past me, sitting on the swing and knocked on the screen door. I sat there all quiet but the swing squeaked. The Shape turned toward me. I didn't know what it was but it was big. . . .
>
> Some of the people in the Circle say El Jefe killed three men in Diablo de Ojo for no more than the cost of a cup of coffee. Say he did it for the crowd . . . them chanting, "Silencio, silencio, Diablo." (1)

When people think of urban, they might not think of a hulking, Mexican prizefighter with one eye covered with a patch and fists the size of bear paws, a behemoth of a man who seemed to all but be escorted by shadows and darkness and strength and beauty. I wanted this kind of unexpected hero to exist for Chula in her part of the city known as the Circle:

> Which was mostly Mexican with a couple of Blacks and Whites squished in one edge. Abuela uesta say when I was little, if you could see the neighborhood from up high, all the buildings make up a circle. That it was a gift to live somewhere so magical. To live somewhere that always meets itself. It didn't seem magical with houses all on top of each other. Most of them with their roofs all sagging, door gates and windows with thick bars. (18–19)

Juxtaposed to Squaretown, where Chula attends junior high, race and class disparities become clear:

> Squaretown, it was about eight blocks from where we lived and those kids living there ain't nothing like us. They came in all colors but smelled like cable TV, camera phones, expensive sneakers, JNCO

> jeans and all the CDs you want. Being a Square means you're always asked questions in class first and you never have to stand at the back of the line at lunch. Most of all, and the thing Circles never forget, being a Square meant you'd never have to wish for nothing 'cause you already got everything or the chances for it. (22–23)

Mexican folklore and urban America set against the realities of race and class and a family in beauty and in crisis give a glimpse of a different kind of city landscape.

Pivoting from the mythical to the realistic, the middle book in my Fat Angie Trilogy, *Fat Angie: Rebel Girl Revolution* (Charlton-Trujillo 2019), embarks on a road trip from the smallness of made-up Dryfalls, Ohio, to very real interstates, state oddities, and finally downtown Cincinnati. Although a book about grief, guilt, body shame, and a family in distress, it's also a celebration of learning to live exactly as who you are.

From Brookpark Skateland in Cleveland to America's Shortest Street to having a picnic at the World's Largest Basket and ending at Fountain Square in Cincinnati, this is a book about setting, about the sounds, smells, tastes, textures of every stop, including a very unsavory restroom:

> Water had overflowed from one of the toilets. It clapped against the bottom of Angie's shoes as she walked. The urinals were filthy with cigarette butts and a couple of crushed beer cans.
>
> The door to the first stall hung off its hinge ever so slightly. Another handwritten sign taped to it read in all capital letters:
>
> **DO NOT FLUSH**
> **FEMININE FEMALE PRODUCTS**
>
> . . . Flies fluttered above the definitely not-flushed toilet. A maxi pad hung over the lip of the seat, as if it were making a desperate attempt to climb out of the bowl. (Charlton-Trujillo 2019, 160–61)[1]

Yes, I've been in this restroom in real time, and yes, it was soooo bad! Shifting to a less disgusting look at life on the road, here's Angie's arrival into the downtown of the Queen City:

> Cincinnati, Ohio, was not Dryfalls. Interstates intersecting with interstates intersecting with more interstates. Cars sometimes swerving in and out of lanes. Headlights and fast-flow traffic. It was more than a Starbucks town. It was an almost-everything town. Stores, stadiums and . . . lights. It had a pulse and an energy. (269)

The chaotic feel of entering Cincinnati directly metaphors Angie's own journey and transformation.

Landscape. It's the space that is around us. The sound, the rhythm, the rhyme. The assonance, the tonality, the texture. The rooftop garden. The b-ballers in the park. The elderly couple, walking their Chihuahua in the dark. It is the red door in Chinatown. The birds chirping, horns honking, airplanes soaring overhead. It is the history of injustice and the opportunities of unlearning. It is this moment of you . . . listening, honing in on the detail of your own story—in verse or prose, in lyrics or spoken word—with thought bubbles and drawings for graphic novels. It is flash fiction, nonfiction—the direction of your story belongs to you. Now tell it. Your way. Your voice.

Find your place in the landscape.

Notes

1. FAT ANGIE: REBEL GIRL REVOLUTION. Copyright © 2019 by e. E. Charlton-Trujillo. Reproduced by permission of the publisher, Candlewick Press, Somerville, MA.

References

Charlton-Trujillo, e.E. 2006. *Prizefighter en Mi Casa*. New York: Delacorte Press.

Charlton-Trujillo, e.E. 2019. *Fat Angie: Rebel Girl Revolution*. Somerville, MA: Candlewick Press.

CHAPTER TWO

Storifying the City: Examining Representations of Urban Areas in Sherri L. Smith's *Orleans*

Sean P. Connors

To call attention to the role that stories play in shaping readers' perceptions of the places where people live, I ask students in a young adult (YA) literature course I teach to reflect on the images and feelings that different places evoke for them. As an example, Arkansas, the state where the majority of my predominantly white middle- to working-class southern students grew up, elicits responses such as the following: "rural," "conservative," "outdoors," "green," "family values," "southern," and "home." The city of Detroit, on the other hand, elicits a less positive set of images, including "car manufacturers," "pollution," "crime," "poverty," "vacant buildings," and "struggle." Asked whether they have ever visited Detroit, the majority of my students indicate that they have not, prompting us to consider how they acquired their knowledge of it. Faced with that question, students describe the role that different media—from film and television to literature, magazines, and music—have played in shaping their perception of what Detroit is like, and they agree that a person from that city would likely tell a different story about it. This exercise also yields interesting results when I ask students to imagine how a person who'd never visited Arkansas might describe the state. Familiar with stereotypes of southern people and places, they are quick to volunteer terms such as "conservative," "Christian fundamentalist," "backward," "poorly educated," and "intolerant."

By engaging students in exercises like this one, I hope to help them understand that places, composed as they are of brick and mortar, are not limited to a material dimension. They also possess a social and a political dimension. To say that places are socially constructed is to say that they acquire meaning, in part, from the stories that different groups of people tell about them. And, of course, there are many, often competing, stories told about a place. As an example, cities are alternatively depicted as centers for art, progressivism, education, cosmopolitanism, and culture and as sites of overcrowding, crime, and pollution. Places are also implicated in power. For example, some cities are considered more important than others, either for social, cultural, or economic reasons, and as such, they are afforded more social status and hence more resources.

In a popular Ted Talk, Chimamanda Adichie (2009) cautions against the dangers of the single story, a term she uses to refer to stories that depict a population of people "as one thing, as only one thing, over and over again." As the classroom exercise described earlier demonstrates, places are the subject of single stories as well. As a form of popular culture, young adult literature constitutes one site where single stories about place are reproduced and resisted.

In this chapter, I present a conceptual framework that teachers can use to support students' attending closely (and critically) to how cities are depicted in YA literature. In the next section, I construct my framework, drawing on the work of scholars who have examined the social and political dimensions of place, and who theorize it as a site of contested meanings. I then apply the framework to Sherri L. Smith's (2013) *Orleans*, a work of YA dystopian fiction that imagines a future where violent hurricanes, coupled with a blood-borne contagion, have led the U.S. government to abandon its interests in the Gulf Coast region, leaving the residents of Orleans (formerly New Orleans), the majority of whom are people of color, to fend for themselves. In doing so, I examine two stories that circulate about the city in the text. The first, told from an outsider's perspective, imagines it as a site of devastation, loss, and danger. The second, told from an insider's perspective, centers on the strength and courage of the people who live in Orleans and finds hope in the city's resilience.

A Framework for Analyzing Representations of Place in YA Literature

What differentiates "space" from "place"? To begin, space is a more abstract concept than place. It is often conceived of as a container in which human activity occurs or as a plane that people cross as they move from one point to another. Place, on the other hand, refers to a specific location in space, one that a person could name and point to on a map. Unlike space, place is imbued with meaning. As Tim Cresswell (2004) argues, "[w]hen humans invest meaning in a portion of space and then become attached to it in some way (naming is one such way) it becomes place" (10).

In her book *For Space*, geographer and social scientist Doreen Massey (2005) theorizes place as a product of human relations, arguing that it is always under construction and hence always undetermined (7). According to Massey, people from different social and cultural backgrounds and with different life trajectories contribute to the production of place as they go about their everyday lives and navigate their "throwntogetherness" (141). Likening the production of place to a ballet, Creswell (2004) argues that "places are performed on a daily basis through people living their everyday life" (34). From this perspective, a person's ability to know a place, or feel a sense of belonging to it, is contingent on their possessing the knowledge needed to participate effectively in its daily routines. On the other hand, "those who do [not] know the routine will appear clumsy and 'out-of-place' simply through the non-conformity of their bodily practice" (Cresswell 2004, 34). Collectively, these arguments indicate that people come to know a place as they interact bodily with its material, social, and political dimensions. The first two questions that teachers and students can ask in the service of analyzing representations of cities in YA literature is thus: *How do the characters in the text acquire their knowledge of the city, and how does this in turn shape their perceptions of it?*

If place is a point in space that people have invested with meaning, it is also a nexus for stories. Massey (2005) links stories to place when she theorizes "space as a simultaneity-of-stories so far" (9). If this is the case, she argues, "then places are collections of those stories, articulations within the wider power-geometries of space" (130). Linda McDowell (1997) also establishes a relationship between stories and place when she argues that "places are both concrete and symbolic. They are literally and metaphorically made up: of buildings, field systems, roads and railways as well as *of* myths and legends, statues and ceremonies that link people to a place" (2). Massey's and McDowell's arguments suggest that to know a place—that is, to acquire the knowledge needed to participate effectively in its routines and practices—involves more than simply becoming acquainted with its built environment. Equally important is "joining up with, somehow linking into, the collection of interwoven stories of which that place is made" (Massey 2005, 119). Massey's comments call attention to the plurality of stories that can circulate about a given place. Thus, another question that teachers and students can ask in the service of analyzing representations of cities in YA literature is, *What stories do characters in the text tell about the city, and how do they portray it?*

As explained earlier, places are implicated in power. According to Bill Green (2012), places are not "positioned equally, or distributed on a level plane, or playing field" (379). Instead, some are afforded more social status than others. Barbara Comber (2016) states the problem more succinctly when she argues that "it is the relationships between people and places that produce poverty and inequities" (7). When investigating how cities are depicted in YA literature, it is therefore necessary to attend closely to the competing stories that characters tell about them. In some cases, these stories may reproduce problematic beliefs and assumptions about cities held by the dominant culture, approximating what Adichie (2019) calls a single story. When this is the case, a text can perpetuate stereotypes about cities and urban dwellers. On the other hand, an author may resist single stories about urban areas and position readers to view them in a way they might not otherwise have considered. A fourth and fifth question that teachers and students can ask in the service of examining representations of cities in YA literature is thus: *Does the text tend to reproduce or resist single stories about cities, and what evidence suggests this?*

Figure 2.1
A Framework for Analyzing Representations of Urban Areas in Young Adult Literature

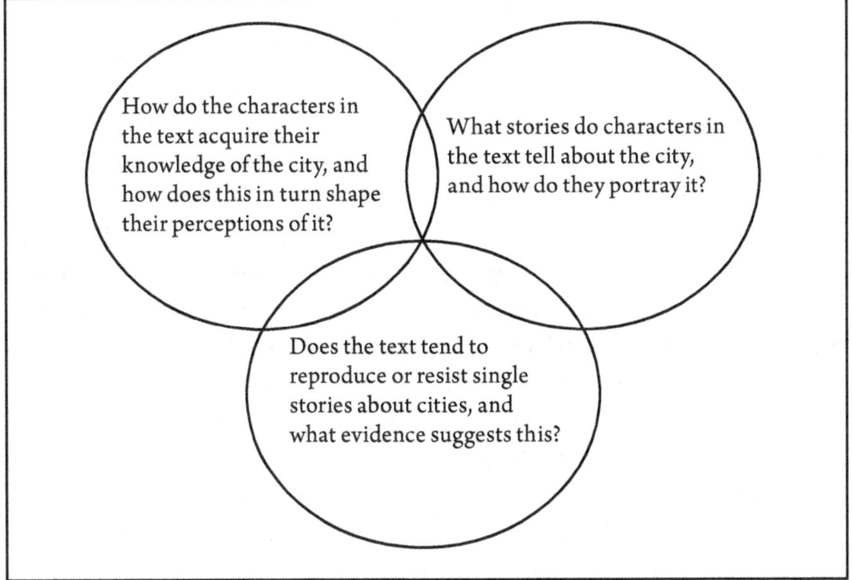

Figure 2.1 presents a framework that teachers and students can use to evaluate whether a work of YA fiction tends to reproduce or resist single stories about cities. In the sections that follow, I apply this framework to Sherri L. Smith's (2013) *Orleans*, a work of YA dystopian fiction that takes place in the future in the city formerly known as New Orleans. As Keith Booker (1994) has argued, dystopian literature has a long tradition of engaging in the project of social criticism, and this is the case with Smith's novel, which can be interpreted as critiquing the federal government's response to Hurricane Katrina in 2005 and the role that structural racism played in allowing the city's most vulnerable populations to suffer in the weeks and months that followed. To accomplish this, the novel positions readers to view the city from the perspectives of an insider and an outsider. In doing so, it invites readers to look past deficit narratives the media perpetuated about New Orleans in the days following Hurricane Katrina and acknowledge the city's strength, beauty, and resilience.

Analyzing Representations of the City in *Orleans*

Orleans (Smith 2013) is set in the future after a series of destructive hurricanes have devastated the city of New Orleans, unleashing a blood-borne contagion known as Delta Fever and prompting the U.S. government to abandon its economic and material interests in the Gulf Coast region. To contain the people of Orleans, the majority of who are people of color, and prevent them from crossing into the Outer States and infecting its populace, the government has constructed a massive border wall that stretches along its southern border and which is patrolled by armed soldiers. Because the severity of Delta Fever differs depending on a person's blood type, the people in the Gulf Coast region have banded together in blood tribes (A, B, AB, O positive, and O negative). When a group of ABs attacks her O-positive tribe, Fen de la Guerre, a seventeen-year-old African American girl and the novel's protagonist, unexpectedly finds herself faced with the prospect of having to rescue a newborn, Baby Girl (later Enola Jeanne Marie), whose mother, the tribe's chieftain, died in childbirth. Having promised to deliver Baby Girl (who is immune to Delta Fever for a brief window of time) over the wall, Fen is unexpectedly assisted by Daniel, a scientist from the Outer States who traveled to Orleans to perfect a cure he has engineered for Delta Fever. In its present form, however, the vaccine threatens to kill anyone infected with the contagion. In exchange for Fen leading him to the former Institute for Post-Separation Studies, where he hopes to find research he can use to perfect his cure, Daniel promises to take Baby Girl with him when he returns to the Outer States.

Outsider versus Insider Knowledge

As seen in Figure 2.1, the first two questions that teachers and students can ask to investigate representations of cities in YA literature are, *How do the characters in the text acquire their knowledge of the city, and how does this, in turn, shape their perceptions of it?* Reflecting his faith in science and objectivity, Daniel's knowledge of Orleans is based on information he has gathered from government maps, research reports, census data, and other official documents. As a scientist employed by the U.S. government, Daniel also has access to an array of expensive technologies. When he travels to Orleans, he does so wearing a hermetically sealed containment suit designed to protect him from contracting Delta Fever. He also wears a datalink, a computer-like device that permits him to access information on any topic simply by asking it a question. Additionally, Daniel places great confidence in the research he assumes the scientists and medical doctors at the former Institute for Post-Separation Studies had conducted in the service of studying Delta Fever. In all these ways, Daniel's knowledge of Orleans is that of the scientist: objective and dispassionate. Indeed, his mission in exploring Orleans is simply "to see it for what it was" (Smith 2013, 109).

Throughout the novel, Daniel's knowledge of Orleans is shown to be faulty. He assumes that "[n]avigating the empty streets of Orleans should be simple enough" (72), but the information he relies on to do so is culled from sources that are in some cases "fifty years out of date" (52). He trusts his datalink to provide him with more accurate maps and data, but the humid environment in the Delta unexpectedly causes the technology to fail. Cut off from the maps he needs to navigate the city, Daniel finds himself lost. Having relied on faulty estimates from the last U.S. census, which put the population of "the Delta region at eight thousand, approximately sixty-five hundred in or near the environs of the former city of New Orleans" (72), he is also surprised to find that, in fact, "the city was alive, and in such variety that it stunned [him]" (153).

Whereas Daniel's knowledge of Orleans is based on information culled from government reports and documents, Fen was born and raised in Orleans, and her knowledge of the city is acquired through lived experience. Unlike Daniel, whose ability to navigate Orleans is contingent on his having access to current maps and expensive technology, Fen's knowledge of the city is embodied. When they visit Rooftops, a section of the city so named because it consists of houses long since buried beneath an avalanche of mud and silt, Fen understands how to walk across the earth without causing a sinkhole to open and swallow her, a mistake that Daniel makes, causing him to lose the cure he had been developing for Delta Fever. When they pass through the AB tribe's territory, Fen understands that the grassy median between two roads constitutes neutral ground, affording her and Daniel a measure of protection that he fails to recognize as an outsider. Even Fen's bodily movements are shaped by knowledge unavailable to Daniel. Studying her as she moved through the woods, he notes, "She didn't stand, but moved in a crouch, wary, *listening for things he couldn't hear. Looking for signs he couldn't read*" (276, emphasis added).

Just as Fen is able to read the woods, she can also read her family's history inscribed in the surrounding landscape, the result of which connects her to it in a way that Daniel is not. When she happens across a small clearing in the woods where she and her parents had once lived, she "walk[s] around the edge of the glade, touch[es] the trees, and remember[s] how Mama had a hammock tied between these two trees on sunny days in the middle of summer, and how Daddy got so angry when he saw me carving my name into that trunk because it be a sign someone live here" (305). In these and other ways, Fen is in synch with her environment, the result of which advantages her. Unlike Daniel, whose status as an outsider exposes him to risk in Orleans, Fen is confident in her ability to survive the city, a fact she attributes to her deep knowledge of it. As she teasingly reminds Daniel, "You got no idea 'bout a lot of things. *You a tourist,* pure and simple" (151, emphasis added).

Competing Stories about the City

Another two questions that teachers and students can ask in the service of investigating how cities are represented in YA literature are, *What stories do characters in the text tell about the city, and how do they portray it?* As explained, Daniel's knowledge of Orleans is cobbled together from stories he collected from government reports and other official documents. As such, it is incomplete. As an outsider, he perceives Orleans as equal parts threatening and exotic. For him, it is a "mysterious, abandoned city," one that had attained a mythical status, "like Shangri-La or Avalon" (51).

Daniel's knowledge of Orleans is comparable to that of a tourist, a point Fen reminds him of throughout the novel. Although he'd never visited the city, Daniel is familiar with the Superdome, "an icon of old New Orleans—the defining silhouette of the city's skyline, the sports stadium that had housed thousands of football games and concerts in its heyday" (106). Likewise, he is familiar with the city's contributions to jazz music, and he recalls having watched footage of second-line funerals on television, a tradition in New Orleans characterized by "cheerful dancing mourners ... [who] carried feathered umbrellas and were led by jazz bands" (108).

A second image that defines Orleans for Daniel is that of the "necropolis." Prior to visiting the city, he had assumed that a series of deadly hurricanes, coupled with a blood-borne contagion, had decimated its population, rendering it "a city of the dead" (109). In his mind, Orleans is little more than a "dead, diseased city" (110), a "dangerous" and "hostile" place (165) "more alien than any place he'd ever been" (146). He is therefore surprised to discover that his story of the city is incomplete. Upon reaching the Superdome, he happens across a group of nuns, the Ursuline Sisters, who had remained in the city at their own peril to care for its dying and dead. Later, when he and Fen visit an encampment of Asian people that had grown up along the Gulf coastline, Daniel is surprised to find that "[f]amilies lived here. Children. Life of a sort he hadn't expected to find. Thriving life" (146). In these ways, accompanying Fen through Orleans problematizes the stories that Daniel had heard about the city. In the end, he is forced to concede that though "the Delta might be dangerous, . . . it was still very much alive" (246).

Like Daniel, Fen is cognizant of the dangers and risks that accompany living in a city devastated by severe weather and contagion. Nevertheless, she is also privy to stories that allow her to appreciate the city's resilience. As explained, in the wake of hurricanes that decimated the city, the people of Orleans, seeking to contain the spread of Delta Fever, banded together in tribes according to blood type. In this tribal society, the responsibility for collecting and preserving each tribe's history falls to storytellers, and stories are the vehicle through which it is passed to future generations. In Fen's O-positive tribe, Cinnamon Jones regales his audiences with stories that recall life in New Orleans before the arrival of hurricanes and Delta Fever. In language that diametrically opposes the terms Daniel uses to describe the city, Jones recalls Orleans as "a beautiful place, a city that sparkled like diamonds, sang like songbirds, and danced a two-step to stop men's hearts" (35). In his stories, the city's beauty is further amplified by its racial diversity:

> Lord, the people. They was black, and white, and yellow, and brown, and pink as a lobster sometimes, too, but they was beautiful. Because they could dance like the city, and sing like the city, and love like the city was loved by the sky and the sea. It was the *people* who made the city of New Orleans. (35)

Just as stories serve to document and preserve Orleans's rich history, they also connect generations. Fen comforts Baby Girl by telling her stories the child's mother, Lydia, once told Fen. She recalls having told those "same stories [to] Lydia while she giving birth" (274). At the center of these stories is the character of Jeanne Marie, a trickster-like figure said to have tricked the devil into giving her back the moon (274). That Fen ultimately names Baby Girl "Enola" (an acronym for East New Orleans, Louisiana) Jeanne Marie is symbolic: just as the people of Orleans embody the city's spirit, Fen regards the child as exemplifying its hope and resilience. To be sure, Fen is well aware of the dangers associated with living in a devastated city, but her stories allow her to understand Orleans as more than that. The city may have befallen hardships, but Fen's stories acknowledge its rich history, diversity, and mythology in ways that Daniel's single story does not.

Reproducing and Resisting Single Stories about Cities

Other questions that teachers and students can ask in the service of examining how cities are depicted in YA literature are, *Does the text tend to reproduce or resist single stories about cities, and what evidence suggests this?* As explained, Adichie defines single stories as stories that depict a population of people "as one thing, as only one thing, over and over again." She argues that like stereotypes, "[t]he problem with [single stories] is not that they are untrue, but that they are incomplete. They make one story become the only story."

In Smith's novel, Daniel's knowledge of Orleans is shaped by a single story. Representations of the city he had encountered in the media, coupled with the government reports he had read (e.g., census reports, statistical data, etc.), lead him to perceive Orleans as a place of danger and contagion, which it is. As the story unfolds, however, Daniel comes to understand that the suffering the people of Orleans endured was exacerbated by structural racism. Fen informs him that though the government had ordered people to evacuate the city in advance of Hurricane Jesus, the most devastating storm, many lacked the means to do so:

> But can't everybody fit on a road out of town at the same time. Some people can't even get up outta they beds, so what *they* gonna do? No

> gas for the cars, and the roads be clogged, and people be needing they medicine and whatnot. . . . The city been full of workers, immigrants who came here for jobs rebuilding since the Government been promising work and all. They stuck here too, living in trailers and cheap housing, what the Government provide. (172)

When they reach the Institute for Post-Separation Studies, Fen tells Daniel that the legions of doctors, researchers, and scientists who had descended on Orleans in the aftermath of Jesus's destruction had not done so out of a noble desire to help the city's people but rather to study how they behaved when blood, rather than race, provided a logic for social hierarchization. In disbelief, Daniel exclaims, "A new form of racism. . . . It's like Tuskegee all over again. They never wanted a cure" (207). Revealing her distrust of social and political institutions that have consistently failed her, Fen reflects, "I don't know nothing about Tuskegee, but if it mean folks with power always gonna abuse it, then I got to agree" (207). Later, Fen and Daniel discover that the government, hoping to reclaim its resources in the delta, is smuggling weapons into the region in an effort to incite genocide. In these ways, *Orleans* positions readers to appreciate the role that structural racism plays in privileging some groups of people (and places) and oppressing others. Hurricanes may have inflicted damage on Orleans, but its fall into ruin is attributable to its having been abandoned by powerful institutions.

Like Daniel, Fen is also cognizant of the dangers that life in Orleans poses, but unlike him, she understands that the city is more than that single story. Equally important are the strength and resilience its people exemplify, a fact she communicates to Daniel (appropriately enough) in the form of a story. On their way to the Institute for Post-Separation Studies, Fen, Baby Girl, and Daniel take refuge in an abandoned building. As they talk, a group of costumed riders on horseback and brandishing torches unexpectedly appears in the street, where they proceed to sing, shout, and perform a series of intricate maneuvers before galloping off into the night. Daniel interprets the riders as a threat to their safety, but Fen explains that what they witnessed was in fact a "krewe" performing a ritual that dates back to the days immediately following Hurricane Jesus. She explains:

> That first year after Jesus, when it been looking like we dead, that when the first krewe start. Somebody found an old Mardi Gras warehouse or something, and he pull out some costumes and go riding through the streets. Just one man holding up a lantern, saying, "We still here, we still here, thank Lord almighty, we still here." I know somebody said he seen the man, riding like a damn fool, chest-deep through the floodwaters. And he couldn't help but follow. And other people started, too, 'til they all been wading along, with they flashlights and dancing, 'cause this be new Orleans and that be what we do," he say. And every year, when the season for storms be over, somebody get out there and take up a torch and find theyselves a horse and do it all over again. (173)

For Daniel, the riders represent a threat. But Fen's knowledge of the city's history, articulated in the form of stories, permits her to interpret their appearance as "a good sign" (171). In this way, a central theme in the novel celebrates the strength and resilience that the people of New Orleans exemplify and the spirit of hope that sustains them, even in difficult times.

Teaching Literature to Disrupt Single Stories about Place

Place matters, as do the stories that people tell about it. On one hand, stories about cities can be stigmatizing. Consider, for example, the vile imagery that Donald Trump's racist characterization of Baltimore as a "disgusting, rat and rodent infested mess" and a place that "no human being would want to live" elicits (McGraw 2019). On the other hand, stories can call attention to the cultural richness and diversity that make a city unique. Ebony Elizabeth Thomas (2011) argues that the "noticings and rememberings" that readers acquire of urban landscapes through literature "contribute to the formation of [their] identities, as well as their sense of being anchored in worlds both fictional and real" (13). Citing Wendy Glenn's (2008) work, however, Thomas also notes that "reading for the role of place and environment is often subordinated by other concerns, such as a focus on identity, ideology, or culture" (14).

Just as teachers expect students to examine how identity categories such as race, gender, social class, religion, and sexuality are depicted in works of

YA literature, they should also ask them to attend closely to how places are represented. Things to Think About presents a series of questions that teachers and students can ask to examine the relationship between story and place before, during, and after reading a work of YA fiction. For teachers interested in learning more about this approach to reading, Things to Explore highlights additional resources, including YA novels that lend themselves to being read from a place-based perspective. By attending closely to how YA literature reproduces and resists single stories about cities, students are better prepared to identify problematic narratives about their own communities and to replace them with stories they know to be more accurate representations.

Things to Think About

Questions to Ask before Reading

1. What stories do students associate with the communities where they live (or the school they attend)?
2. What stories do students suspect an outsider might tell about their local community (or school)? What stories might a member of the local community (or school) tell about it? How do students account for differences between these two sets of stories?
3. In what ways are stories about place productive? How can they result in problems or misunderstandings?

Questions to Ask while Reading

1. How do characters in the book describe their local community? In what terms do people outside of the community perceive or describe it?
2. How does the community where a story is set impact how characters perceive or understand the world?

3. How does the community where a story is set reaffirm stories told about it? In what ways does it problematize or resist those stories?

Questions to Ask after Reading

1. What does it mean to know a place?
2. How is power implicated in the way that different places are perceived or understood?
3. Can students think of occasions when people have told problematic narratives about their local community? How do they understand their local communities to problematize or resist those stories?

Things to Explore

1. **de la Peña, Matt, and Christian Robinson. *Last Stop on Market Street*. New York: G. P. Putnam's Sons, 2015.** In this beautifully written and illustrated picturebook, CJ accompanies his grandmother on a bus ride across the city. During their trip, they share different perspectives on the neighborhoods they pass through and the people they encounter. CJ's grandmother helps CJ to appreciate the beauty to be found in unexpected places if only when one is willing to look.
2. **Thomas, Ebony Elizabeth. "Landscapes of City and Self: Place and Identity in Urban Young Adult Literature." *The ALAN Review* 38, no. 2 (2011): 13–22.** This article examines how urban landscapes are alternatively depicted as geographies of privilege and geographies of challenge in YA literature. In addition to examining works of YA fiction that reproduce these tropes, the author highlights a series of novels in which the two geographies intersect.
3. **Zoboi, Ibi. *Pride*. New York: Balzer + Bray, 2018.** In this YA adaptation of Jane Austen's *Pride and Prejudice*, seventeen-year-

old Zuri Benitez is proud of her Brooklyn neighborhood, but she worries about the impact urban gentrification will have on the community she knows and loves. Her concerns are exacerbated when the wealthy Darcy family moves into a renovated home adjacent to the apartment building where Zuri and her family live.

References

Adichie, Chimamana. 2009. "The Danger of a Single Story." *TED*, uploaded by TEDGlobal, July, video file, 8:34. http://www.ted.com/talks/chimamanda_adichie_the_danger_of_a_single_story.html.

Booker, Keith M. 1994. *The Dystopian Impulse in Modern Literature: Fiction as Social Criticism*. Westport, CT: Greenwood.

Comber, Barbara. 2016. *Literacy, Place, and Pedagogies of Possibility*. New York: Routledge.

Cresswell, Tim. 2004. *Place: A Short Introduction*. Chichester, UK: Blackwell.

Glenn, Wendy. 2008. "Gossiping Girls, Insider Boys, A-list Achievement: Examining and Exposing Young Adult Novels Consumed by Conspicuous Consumption." *Journal of Adolescent and Adult Literacy* 52(1): 34–42.

Green, Bill. 2012. "Literacy, Place and the Digital World." *Language and Education* 26(4): 377–82.

Massey, Doreen. 2005. *For Space*. Thousand Oaks, CA: Sage Publications.

McDowell, Linda. 1997. "Introduction: Rethinking Place." In *Undoing Place?: A Geographical Reader*, edited by Linda McDowell, 1–12. Abingdon, UK: Routledge.

McGraw, Meredith. 2019. "President Trump Heads to Baltimore, a City He Called a 'Rodent Infested Mess.'" ABC News, September 12. https://abcnews.go.com/Politics/president-trump-heads-baltimore-city-called-rodent-infested/story?id=65570278.

Smith, Sherri L. 2013. *Orleans*. New York: Penguin.

Thomas, Ebony Elizabeth. 2011. "Landscapes of City and Self: Place and Identity in Urban Young Adult Literature." *The ALAN Review* 38(2): 13–22.

CHAPTER THREE

GENRE AND GENTRIFICATION IN THE YOUNG ADULT NOVEL

Karen Coats

AS I PLANNED what was to be my final syllabi for my young adult (YA) literature classes at Illinois State University, I aimed for as much diversity as I could pack into a fifteen-week semester. In addition to considering representations of various identities and avoiding a "single story" with regard to those representations, I wanted my students, most of whom were going to be secondary English/ Language Arts teachers, to analyze the elements and conventions of different literary forms, such as verse novels and graphic narratives; modes (conceived as attitudes toward the content), including tragicomedy, horror, satire, and melodrama; and popular YA genres, such as character-driven psychological realism, contemporary adaptations of traditional stories, and fantasy. I structured the course so that the first discussions of the books were entirely student-led; following their lead, then I picked up and extended the threads that they found most important and relevant to their understanding of the texts as well as to their lives. Interestingly, my students located a motif linking two very different novels set in urban environments—gentrification.

Gentrification is a process whereby working-class neighborhoods are overtaken by an influx of middle- and upper-class-owned businesses and property developers who benefit from tax incentives to renovate existing structures, often forcing lifetime residents to move because they can no longer afford to live there; because of this displacement, it is almost always thought of in negative terms. Considering that my students saw gentrification in both books, which were the only two in the course set in cities, I began to wonder: Is gentrification becoming part of a "single story" about life in the city? Only one of the books, Renée Watson's (2015) *This Side of Home*, has an explicit focus on the attitudes of the characters toward their gentrifying neighborhood. But the students who led the discussion on another book, Daniel José Older's (2015) *Shadowshaper*, made a direct connection between the Brooklyn setting of that book and what was happening in their own Chicago neighborhood of Pilsen. In our follow-up discussion of these two novels, we analyzed the ways in which an urban setting factors into constructing particular kinds of narrative situations and conflicts. But their presentation also got me thinking about other books where gentrification plays either an implicit or explicit role in the plots of YA novels set in cities: What stories do these books tell, and how does the author's choice and handling of genre conventions suggest a perspective on the topic?

In this chapter then, I explore ways we can help students consider how various genres use their urban settings to convey a particular attitude toward a pressing issue of life in a modern city. In addition to Watson's and Older's texts, I will discuss *Monday's Not Coming*, a tragic mystery and realistic crime drama with an unreliable narrator by Tiffany D. Jackson (2018); and *Revolution*, a mixed-genre work by Jennifer Donnelly (2010). My focus is on gentrification, but there are, of course, other topics in urban literature, including these novels, that could be approached through a study of genre conventions, such as gender identity, violence, immigration, adolescence, mental health, abuse, and intersectionality, among others. For the teen characters in the novels under discussion here, however, the material and metaphorical effects of gentrification constitute a special case whether they are foregrounded or form a significant backdrop to the events that unfold. Interestingly, however, the focalizing character in each of these novels is economically well situated; the characters in danger of eviction due to urban renewal projects are either close friends or people they see regularly as they walk around their urban neighborhoods. This situation thus allows some critical distance for characters to see how and why their neighborhoods are changing even though they themselves aren't the ones being displaced. By pulling back even further into a discussion of how genre conventions subtly direct their expectations and interpretations, readers can reflect on how a book might point them toward a broader moral response to what gentrification means and how it affects communities and individuals, as each genre hails, according to Chandler, its "'ideal reader,' including their attitudes towards the subject matter and often their class, age, gender and ethnicity" (Sabao 2014, 4). The gentrifying city signifies not only the physical loss of home for some of the characters but also a sense of disempowerment in the face of political and economic circumstances and the threat of displacement from or the dissolution of a cultural community central to their identity. Such concerns are of course central to YA literature because they are core concerns of adolescents themselves as they prepare to leave home and craft identities of choice amid uncertain economic times. How they are represented in various genres both reflects and helps shape attitudes toward the factors that affect teen identity in a contemporary urban environment.

A Few Words on Gentrification

The novels I have chosen to discuss are set in cities that rank among the top ten places that have seen a significant displacement of black and Latinx residents due to a process of outside investors taking advantage of low property values and government-supported revitalization projects (Richardson, Mitchell, and Franco 2019). The term *gentrification* was coined by sociologist Ruth Glass in 1964 to describe the transformations of certain working-class London neighborhoods into enclaves affordable only to the wealthy. Although "Glass's description of gentrification would transcend its origins, becoming shorthand for the spatialization of class struggle" (Subramanian 2020), the process in the United States was understood from the start as deliberately racialized as well, with James Baldwin calling urban renewal in 1960s' San Francisco "negro removal" (Graham 2015), and bell hooks (2000) referring to it in 1990 as "state-orchestrated, racialized class warfare . . . taking place all around the United States" (137). In *This Side of Home*, Watson (2015) shares a similar view when Maya, the narrator, learns the history of her Portland neighborhood from an older man named Mr. Washington: "He tells me that in the seventies hundreds of homes were destroyed so that the hospital could expand. An urban renewal project, they called it. Displaced a lot of families. Most of us black, you know" (263).

Although gentrification is not the main theme of *Monday's Not Coming* (Jackson 2018), it forms a recurrent thread throughout the novel. Narrator Claudia relates the history of the Washington, D.C., housing project where her best friend, Monday, lives—a place Claudia's middle-class parents don't allow her to visit alone:

> The Capitol Housing Authority built the Edward Borough housing projects during World War II on land originally given to freed slaves during the 1800s. It was meant to be a place of community, a place to start again, a place for the American dream.
>
> Later on, developers realized how valuable the land was, sitting right on the river, with easy access to the city. Too valuable for black folks to have. . . .
>
> Everyone's afraid of Ed Borough, while Ed Borough should have been afraid of everyone else. (38)

When Monday disappears, Claudia insists that her mother take her to see Monday's mother, who resents this intrusion into her privacy but clearly fears for her family's future:

> Mrs. Charles shrugged, her lips turning up. "Oh, you know. Keep on keeping on, I guess. You heard about them trying to kick everybody out around here? They want to bulldoze the whole neighborhood and build condos for white folks. People already started getting them eviction notices." (105)

Although Mrs. Charles adamantly refuses to make excuses for the tragedy that unfolds, the pointed comments about how "[t]his city has it out bad for us. . . . Rather throw us all out and start with a clean slate than fix a broken toilet" (188), and the protests that are ultimately unsuccessful in saving Ed Borough that appear throughout the story suggest that her distress was exacerbated by the very real threat of homelessness and the destruction of their community.

In *Revolution* (Donnelly 2010), gentrification plays an even smaller role that nevertheless has similar ripple effects of violence. Main character Andi is an upper-class white Manhattanite who passes a derelict hotel on her way to school every day with her younger brother. Having fallen into disrepair, the hotel "house[s] welfare cases and winos," including a schizophrenic man named Max (20). Aware that the hotel is due for renovation, Max goes on regular tirades about "the mayor, the housing commission, and Donald Trump," but the day he is served with his eviction notice so that developers can proceed with their revitalization project, he becomes especially violent, grabbing Andi's little brother, Truman, and running into the street where they are both killed by a delivery van (367). In both these books, then, the protagonists lose someone dear to them at the hands of a mentally unstable person who is being threatened with this loss of their home. Although their mental illnesses are the proximate cause of the tragedies, the impending loss of home is not incidental as a thematic element, as the protagonists themselves subsequently experience displacement within their own minds. Claudia suffers traumatic amnesia when she realizes what has happened to Monday, losing three years of her life. Andi also experiences a significant break with reality which can be read either as a time-travel fantasy or a hallucination brought on by mixing antidepressants, alcohol, and a head injury. Although the girls' domestic situations distance them from the effects of gentrification, the authors bring in reminders of it whenever Claudia and Andi tell the stories of their respective traumas, thus intimating that it was at least a partial trigger for the characters' ultimate breakdowns.

Gentrification can thus factor in YA novels as a secondary or symbolic element as well as a material one. My students immediately picked up on the fact that the Bedford-Stuyvesant neighborhood depicted in *Shadowshaper* (Older 2015) was in danger of gentrification because of two emblematic signifiers: an unfinished building project and vanishing street murals. The opening description of the building project sets the thematic stage:

> The Tower has shown up just over a year ago, totally unannounced: a five-story concrete monstrosity on a block otherwise full of brownstones. The developers built the outer structure quickly and then left

> it, abandoned and unfinished, its unpaned windows staring emptily out into the Brooklyn skies. The Tower's northern wall sat right on the edge of the Junklot, where mountains of trashed cars waited like crumpled-up scraps of paper. Manny and the other old guys who played dominos in the lot had immediately declared war on it. (2)

The fact that the building appeared without warning suggests that there was no community input regarding the project. Its position next to a junk lot reminds readers of the urban blight that likely prompted city officials to approve the project as an attempt at revitalization, but the fact that this lot was a gathering place for older community members and that they "immediately declared war" on the intrusion implies that they did not share the perspective that the neighborhood needed such outside intervention and "renewal." We're not given to know why the project was abandoned, but its presence as an empty, personified monster acts as both symbol and foreshadowing of the climactic action that will take place there.

What we do know is that public murals play a significant role in resisting the encroaching takeover of their neighborhood. Street art is a point of pride in many urban communities, showcasing the talent of individuals who are often disenfranchised from the elite art scene. They are prevalent in Latinx neighborhoods, where the goal is in part to "unify, inspire and educate Mexican-American residents about their proud heritage" (WTTW n.d.) and encourage creativity and expression as positive outlets for young people. Street artists portray the character of their communities through memorial portraits, depictions of significant moments in the history of the community or ethnic group, and scenes that honor the living residents as well as their ancestral heritage.

The murals often function as protests against social injustice as well; for instance, artists in Germany have taken direct aim at real estate developers by depicting them as sharks turned into fish sticks and Dobermans emerging out of doorways (Bross 2017, 4). While Sierra and her friends poke fun at the overpriced coffee and hipster patrons of the new cafes in their neighborhood, Manny, the writer, editor, and publisher of the neighborhood newspaper, commissions Sierra to paint a huge mural on the Tower as part of their war against it. Meanwhile, however, she notices that other murals, including the memorial portraits of an older man and a boy shot by police, are fading. In the real world of

Pilsen, a neighborhood of Chicago, murals are literally disappearing as a result of developers buying and razing the buildings on which they appear. Older's symbolic reference to this real-world effect of gentrification becomes linked to both the horror of ethnic erasure and the triumph of resistance.

Unfortunately, that ambivalence maps onto what actually happens when young people are encouraged to improve their urban environments through artistic expression. Artist and activist Tyler Denmead chronicles the problem in depth through a retrospective study he performed on an arts center he founded called New Urban Arts. As a privileged white creative, he sought to pay his good fortune forward by creating a center for underserved young people in Providence, Rhode Island. Supported by government plans to transform Providence into a "Creative Capital," he was successful insofar as the center has become a haven for young artists. However, his efforts have resulted in the neighborhood becoming an attractive destination for other affluent, mostly white creatives, which has led to the kind of urban renewal and upscale housing costs that have priced out the families of the very young people he hoped to help; in the starkest terms, they have been displaced from the neighborhood they made attractive through their creative labor. Taking into consideration how gentrification deeply affects individuals through the loss of their homes, therefore, it becomes imperative to draw attention to the subtext of gentrification in *Monday's Not Coming* (Jackson 2018) and *Revolution* (Donnelly 2010). Otherwise, the risk is that readers will simply pathologize Monday's mother and Max as deeply disturbed individuals "rather than troubling the unequal and unjust material and symbolic conditions . . . that have produced the trouble they have experienced" (Denmead 2019, 6). But also considering the findings of Denmead's (2019) ethnographic study, Older's (2015) fantastic version of how young people save their own community using their creative talents is revealed to be just that—a fantasy, which leads us to think about how an author's choice of genre relates to the topic of gentrification.

Genre Matters

This Side of Home (Watson 2015) is a densely realistic, contemporary novel that features twin sisters Maya and Nikki and their best friend, Essence, coming to terms with a series of changes in their lives. These rising high school seniors have always lived directly across the street from each other in a working-class neighborhood in Portland, Oregon. Recently, however, the neighborhood is changing, with "new pretty houses and shops that line Jackson Avenue . . . [and] more white families" moving in (4). One result is that Essence is forced to move because rising property values have prompted her landlord to renovate their house and sell it. The influx of nonblack people into their neighborhood has changed the demographics of their school as well, causing their principal to replace their long-standing tradition of a Black History Month celebration with a "diversity assembly" (172), which Maya, the narrator, objects to not only because it was a unilateral decision made by the principal without consulting the students but also because she wants people to focus specifically on the positive contributions made by black people to her neighborhood and the country at large.

Shadowshaper (Older 2015) is an urban fantasy novel dominated by horror elements. The main character, Sierra, comes from a long line of Puerto Ricans who have the ability to call ancestral spirits into material existence by drawing or painting a form for them and inviting them to inhabit the shape to do the bidding of the "shadowshaper." She has been denied her heritage, however, by her *abuelo*, Lázaro, who insisted that the power to shadowshape be limited to the males in the family after her *abuela* refused to use her stronger powers in the way Lázaro wanted her to. Wick, a white anthropologist interested in the occult, infiltrated Lázaro's group of shadowshapers and sought to take it over as their leader. He was convinced that they weren't using the full extent of their powers and that he could do much more by using human corpses rather than drawings as containers for the spirits. As key members of her community die and their decaying bodies are animated under Wick's control, Sierra must learn to use her own powers as a shadowshaper and eventually as their leader to defeat Wick.

In discussing these two novels at the level of genre, the first critical question I posed for my students was this: What sort of moral universes, character constellations, and conflicts do you expect to find in a particular genre? In a fantasy/horror novel, the answer is usually pretty clear: there is a supernatural evil that requires human intervention, augmented by supernatural abilities, to stop its plans. Although it may be difficult at first to identify which characters are on which side and their arcs of growth may involve switching sides as they learn more about what's at stake, the binary moral distinction between good and evil is unambiguous. The fantasy genre highlights this lack of ambiguity insofar as it calls attention to the fact that this story is a product of the imagination; it's not *real,* so it can either be dismissed as "just a story" or its metaphorical character can invite scrutiny as to whether the comparison it appears to be drawing rings true on an abstract level. Realism poses more complicated challenges for critical reading. Events in human experience have consequences that we can only evaluate fairly in retrospect. However, when those events are "emplotted" into a storied account, the author's perspective consciously or unconsciously dominates the narrative. But it is the metonymic character of *realism as a genre*—that is, the sense that this individual story represents commonly experienced realities because of its setting or its use of real-world references—that often results in a "single story" mind-set. In other words, the feeling of reality in this story leads to the belief that it represents the probable truth of all people in similar circumstances.

To the less critical reader, then, realism can appear to be nothing more or less than a direct mirror of reality that requires affirmation or desire in response rather than a genre that "*constrains* the possible ways in which a text is interpreted, guiding readers of a text toward a *preferred reading* (which is normally in accordance with the dominant ideology)" (Chandler 2000, 8) and therefore unlikely to be noticed as an effect of the author's manipulation of the conventions of the genre itself.

In seeking a work of contemporary realism with a multiracial, multiethnic cast of characters, I chose *This Side of Home* (Watson 2015) precisely because the novel presents a remarkably even-handed perspective on urban life rather than guiding readers toward a single viewpoint. Maya and Nikki have different opinions about the changes in their neighborhood. Nikki enjoys shopping at the new boutiques and trying the unfamiliar cuisines of the restaurants that have opened up. She also likes the improved safety of their neighborhood. Maya, on the other hand, admits that her neighborhood has its problems with violence but insists that "[t]here's always been something good here. People just have to open their minds to see it" (4). She laments that none of the new businesses are owned by black people and that the home of an elderly neighbor is now a hipster coffee shop.

By choosing to use twins as characters, Watson (2015) enables readers to consider the good and bad effects of gentrification. She produces what literary theorist Mikhail Bakhtin (1981) calls a dialogic novel, which is one wherein opposing viewpoints are voiced through characters, allowing readers the opportunity to make up their own minds about the subjects of the characters' discourse. A truly dialogic novel is a hard thing to pull off, however, as it's hard to create likable characters who hold opinions the author disagrees with. Readers may argue that because Maya is the narrator, her voice is the strongest one in the novel, and clearly, the principal is not named Mr. Green by accident, as he seems more motivated by mercenary goals than a genuine desire for social justice. But Watson uses details and plot points judiciously: readers will likely be sympathetic to Nikki's desire to be her own person when Essence's cousins berate her for acting white, and Maya's attraction to Tony, her new white neighbor, develops slowly on the basis of shared interests and respect rather than an immediate physical spark. So, in this case, realism works more like reality itself in terms of constructing a messy universe where moral certainties and binary positions are tested and challenged.

The most obvious evidence of a dialogic argument regarding gentrification in *This Side of Home* (Watson 2015) comes through the voice of Mr. Washington. Mr. Washington functions as an elder historian, which is a common enough character type in African American literature to qualify as a generic convention seldom found in white YA literature. He suggests that Maya take a long view of what's happening in her neighborhood by first explaining to her the meaning of the symbol on her necklace, a bird that is "the Adinkra symbol from Ghana. Sankofa. . . . It means 'return and get it'" (262). He reveals to her the struggles black citizens in Portland have endured throughout the twentieth century before finally commenting on the current situation:

> "Most of these folk are just good people trying to make a livin', I suppose. If having them here means more stop signs and handicapped-accessible sidewalks, then so be it. Those of us black folk who do own our homes, who aren't itching to sell, have seen the value of our property rise. It's not all bad. Nothing ever is," Mr. Washington says. "Now, just looking at it from a business standpoint – they need us and

> we need them. They need us to come in to their stores, and we need them to come out into the community and get involved." (267–68)

Such a nuanced perspective on the effects of gentrification stands in sharp contrast with the monologic view put forth in *Monday's Not Coming* (Jackson 2018). The narrator, unreliable though she is, speaks with the same voice as all the other characters when it comes to the destruction of Ed Borough. Similarly, in *Revolution* (Donnelly 2010), although no character other than Max speaks out about the proposed urban renewal project, the connection of Andi's brother's death to Max's eviction marks gentrification as the precipitator of nothing but horrific tragedy and loss. Ultimately, then, we might follow Carolyn Miller's (1984) advice that "a rhetorically sound definition of genre must be centered not on the substance or form of the discourse but on the action it is used to accomplish" (151) and make a distinction between dialogic realism, which seeks to present multiple perspectives, and monologic realism, which functions as an "agent . . . of ideological closure" (O'Sullivan et al. 2004, 128).

As noted earlier, a horror novel like *Shadowshaper* (Older 2015) is less burdened with the obligation for nuanced representations. Although some horror novels do complicate their villains, more often, the conventions of the genre call for a clear enemy with no redeeming characteristics, and Wick certainly fills that role. His motives are as impure as his methods, and real death and destruction follow in his wake. *Shadowshaper* is thus monologic in Bakhtinian terms, figuring Wick's infiltration into the community as an unambivalent threat that must be resisted and beaten back. Older's genre choice of urban fantasy wherein supernatural horror invades a realistic urban setting underwrites his ideological view on the intrusive and destructive effects of gentrification.

The fact that the final showdown between Wick and Sierra takes place in the empty Tower reinforces the point that the crux of the problem is the attempted appropriation and takeover of a Latinx community by a soulless white man who disrespects the history and traditions of the culture. Wick thus represents colonizing white-settler cultures more broadly in their beliefs that they can "improve" upon the cultures they infiltrate. More pointedly, however, he is emblematic of the wealthy, highly educated white people who move in to areas like New York's Bed-Stuy, Chicago's Pilsen, and Providence, Rhode Island, raising property values while destroying the spirit of community identity exemplified and memorialized by the murals.

Avoiding a Single Story of Gentrification and Genre

Most readers begin texts with expectations and opinions about literary genres they prefer or dislike. Many in my young adult literature class also came to our readings and discussions with opinions about gentrification already formed based on prior reading and their own experiences. Through the analysis of gentrification by way of genre, we were able to identify the subtle ways in which generic conventions and expectations manipulate our interpretations of topics as well as our appreciation of a novel. Students who were not fans of horror but who did see gentrification as destructive, for instance, found common cause as they read *Shadowshaper* (Older 2015). Their affective responses were affirmed and amplified by the connection between horror as a genre and the fear of displacement and loss of community that gentrification has come to signify for them; that is, gentrification *is* horror, so that genre is an honest vehicle for its representation. But whether they had given thought to gentrification or not, they were also forced to confront the idea that by framing effective resistance in and as a supernatural fantasy, the text might be suggesting that their power to make real, effective change is only possible in an imaginary world.

Although we didn't read *Monday's Not Coming* (Jackson 2018) or *Revolution* (Donnelly 2010) that semester, I suspect their genre-induced attitudes might have been even more despairing, as these two texts purvey realistic stories of ongoing trauma in the aftermath of loss. All three texts thus present a single story regarding gentrification: it's always destructive to both individuals and communities but is disproportionately so to poor residents of black and Latinx neighborhoods. *This Side of Home* (Watson 2015), by contrast, uses dialogic realism to tell the story of gentrification differently. Through the strategic use of characters who voice opposing perspectives and situations that clearly demonstrate the negative aspects of gentrification but make room for potential positive effects as well, Watson offers readers the opportunity to make up their own minds, or, alternately, keep their minds open about this pressing issue facing all of us but especially teens growing up in the city. If our goal is to help our students become critical readers with strong analytical skills, helping them understand how genres work to shape interpretations of and attitudes toward the subjects they embed is a good place to start.

Things to Think About

1. What genres do you most enjoy reading? What genres do you avoid or dislike? Why do you think this is so?
2. What values, worldviews, and core beliefs inform those genres? How do these values resonate with or inform your own?
3. What expectations do you have for a "good" YA novel that focuses on social justice issues? How might these be different from expectations you might have for other genres and themes?

Things to Explore

1. How has gentrification affected a city near you or the one you live in? Consider videos like this one on YouTube: https://youtu.be/VozAvlmzDFc.
2. Seek out a longtime resident of your neighborhood and inquire about his or her impressions on how the neighborhood has changed and why. CNN has a video that follows the consequences of gentrification on a city's citizens: https://youtu.be/p9eG-wUA8u8.
3. Interview an architect or muralist to investigate their motivations and goals for redesigning public spaces. Find videos on YouTube in which artists are interviewed for their perspectives on whether they have a role to play in the frequency of gentrification. Of possible interest https://www.youtube.com/watch?v=QVBLp4SE-TM.

References

Bakhtin, M. M. 1981. *The Dialogic Imagination: Four Essays*. Edited by Michael Holquist. Translated by Caryl Emerson and Michael Holquist. Austin: University of Texas Press.

Bross, Fabian. 2017. "Beer Prices Correlate with the Quality of Illegal Urban Art: A Case Study on the Relationship Between Street Art and Gentrification in a Berlin Neighborhood." Unpublished manuscript. Accessed March 21, 2020. https://www.academia.edu/33405765/Beer_Prices_Correlate_with_the_Quality_of_Illegal_Urban_Art._A_Case_Study_on_the_Relationship_Between_Street_Art_and_Gentrification_in_a_Berlin_Neighborhood.

Chandler, Daniel. 2000. "An Introduction to Genre Theory." http://visual-memory.co.uk/daniel/Documents/intgenre/chandler_genre_theory.pdf.

Denmead, Tyler. 2019. *The Creative Underclass: Youth, Creativity, and the Gentrifying City*. Durham, NC: Duke University Press.

Donnelly, Jennifer. 2010. *Revolution*. New York: Random House.

Graham, Vince. 2015. *Urban Renewal... Means Negro Removal. James Baldwin (1963)*. Uploaded June 3. Video file. 1:14. https://www.youtube.com/watch?v=T8Abhj17kYU.

hooks, bell. 2000. *Where We Stand: Class Matters*. New York: Routledge.

Jackson, Tiffany D. 2018. *Monday's Not Coming*. New York: HarperCollins.

Miller, Carolyn. 1984. "Genre as Social Action." *Quarterly Journal of Speech* 70(2): 151–67.

Older, Daniel José. 2015. *Shadowshaper*. New York: Scholastic.

O'Sullivan, Tim, John Hartley, Danny Saunders, Martin Montgomery, and John Fiske. 2004. *Key Concepts in Communication and Cultural Studies*. 2nd ed. New York: Routledge.

Richardson, Jason, Bruce Mitchell, and Juan Franco. 2019. *Shifting Neighborhoods: Gentrification and Cultural Displacement in American Cities*. Washington, DC: National Community Reinvestment Coalition. http://ncrc.org/gentrification/.

Subramanian, Divya. 2020. "Ruth Glass: Beyond Gentrification." *New York Review of Books*, January 20. www.nybooks.com/daily/2020/01/20/ruth-glass-beyond-gentrification/.

Watson, Renée. 2015. *This Side of Home*. New York: Bloomsbury.

WTTW Chicago. N.d. "Gallery of Pilsen Murals." Accessed March 21, 2020. https://interactive.wttw.com/my-neighborhood/pilsen/murals.

CHAPTER FOUR

Tears on Concrete: Shaping Youth Identities in the Shadows of Gentrification in Daniel José Older's *Shadowshaper*

Tricia M. Kress and Patricia Patrissy

> *Sierra looked back at the mural . . . a single tear glistened at the corner of Paper Acevedo's painted eyes. The tear wasn't moving—of course it wasn't moving: It was paint! But still: It hadn't been there yesterday or the day before.*
>
> —OLDER (2015, 1)

In Daniel José Older's (2015) *Shadowshaper*, a young adult novel set in Brooklyn, the reader is drawn into the life and vibrancy of New York City through the mural of Papa Acevedo. The larger-than-life painting is a touchstone: Papa Acevedo is a deceased community elder who has been memorialized, smiling, over the Bed-Stuy neighborhood where he lived. But Papa Acevedo's face has been changing. First, he began crying and, eventually fading, revealing the eroding connection between urban community, urban elders, colonial and transmigration lineages, urban youth, and urban land. Papa Acevedo's fading image captures the grief of losing one's community to the forces of gentrification.

This chapter presents Daniel José Older's *Shadowshaper* as an alternative to literature that presents flattened tropes of urban youth and urban spaces. *Shadowshaper* illustrates how urban youth are deeply bound to their communities and the urban landscape via family, history, and the geography of the built and natural environment. Older's complex rendering of urban life can work to combat the ideological erasure of black, brown, and lower-income people who reside in cities, encouraging teachers and students to envision urban youth in fuller renderings that are variegated, vibrant, and situated within the histories and geographies of unique urban lifeworlds. In the following sections, the authors provide a description of the complex rendering of the city in *Shadowshaper* followed by a discussion of how the social construction of person in relation to place contributes to and can combat ideologies that justify displacing urban dwellers and their communities to clear the way for gentrification of urban land. Using illustrations from *Shadowshaper*, the authors demonstrate how urban youth and their environment are deeply bound by interlocking social, historical, and cultural identities.

Shadowshaper: Experiencing the Complexity of the City through Sierra's Quest

Shadowshaper (Older 2015) is a young adult fantasy set in contemporary Brooklyn. It is the first in a three-part series that chronicles the experiences of Sierra, an Afro-Latina of Puerto Rican descent, as she discovers her family's legacy of "shadowshaping." Throughout the narrative arc, Sierra's quest takes her through various locations in New York City: the corner stores of Bed-Stuy, the regal brownstones of Park Slope, the amusement park and beach of Coney Island, and the majestic and manicured campus of Columbia University. Throughout Sierra's journey, the reader experiences the incredibly rich and variegated geographic landscape of New York City, and with it, the complex and variegated relationships that urban young people have with their cities.

The reader is first introduced to Sierra as she is painting a mural for her friend Manny, an adult member of her community. The mural is a giant dragon that stands in defiance of the "Tower," a new high-rise luxury apartment building that has stalled in the construction phase and remains partially constructed and vacant. Through Sierra's eyes, the Tower foreshadows the threat of gentrification and community displacement:

> The Tower had shown up just over a year ago, totally unannounced: a five-story concrete monstrosity on a block otherwise full of brownstones. The developers built the outer structure quickly and then left it, abandoned and unfinished, its unpaned windows staring emptily out into the Brooklyn skies. (2)

The vacant, unfinished, Tower stands in contrast to the fullness of both the brownstones, where neighborhood residents live, and "the Junklot," where Sierra begins her quest and paints her dragon mural: "The Tower's northern wall sat right on the edge of the Junklot, where mountains of trashed cars waited like crumpled up scraps of paper. Manny and the other old guys who played dominos in the lot had immediately declared war on it" (2). From an outside perspective, urban spaces like the Junklot are eyesores, filled with trash and useless, broken things. Yet, the Junklot is also full of life and community knowledge as the elder men of the community gather to play dominoes and share neighborhood stories with others. Manny, in particular, is an important neighborhood figure because he is the editor of an underground neighborhood newspaper.

In contrast, the Tower is invasive in its emptiness, disrupting the neighborhood landscape itself, which Sierra's friend Manny describes in this way: "It's the wall I think that bothers me the most. . . . We used to be able to see all the way down the block, past Carlos's Corner Store to the church, and then down beyond that to the hospital. ¿Ahora? Carajo. The blankness of void vacant estupid" (35–36). The placement of the Tower in the middle of the neighborhood literally divides neighborhood residents from one another. The Tower is an ever-present black hole in the center of the neighborhood. It interrupts the line of sight from one side of the neighborhood to the other. Appropriately, it also serves as the site of the final showdown between Sierra and her friends and the story's primary antagonist.

The start of the novel draws the reader into the primary conflict of the story, but it also introduces the reader to the vibrancy of pre-gentrification Bed-Stuy. Older describes the richness of summertime and sundown in Brooklyn: "Outside, streetlights blinked to life along the streets of Bed-Stuy as the swirling orange clouds gave way to dark blue. All over Brooklyn, folks were heading out to their stoops and strolling the avenues to take in another warm New York night" (6). Sierra's neighborhood is alive, painted in bright colors, with neighborhood residents moving about and enjoying the evening. We see this same vibrancy as Sierra and Bennie are on their way to a party in another neighborhood: "They were fast-walking down Lafayette toward downtown Brooklyn. Some little kids zipped past on scooters. A group of middle-aged women sat in lawn chairs outside a brownstone, sipping beers and laughing" (12). The reader is introduced to the joy and movement of daily neighborhood life as Sierra knows it, with generations of people sharing in community at the end of the day.

As the plot advances, Sierra learns about shadowshaping, which is the supernatural ability to invoke ancestral spirits (i.e., shadows) through art, such as painting and storytelling. Sierra's quest eventually leads to her becoming the bearer of her maternal grandmother's powerful spiritual gift, which many neighborhood residents also share. The reader learns through her emerging friendship and romance with Robbie, a young man of Haitian descent and a shadowshaper, that their community has had a long history of shadowshaping. Sierra's grandfather Abuelo Lazero was also part of a shadowshaper collective; he was one of the most powerful shadowshapers who could invoke the shadows with only his words. Sierra's *abuela*, also known as the shadowshapers' "Lucera," was the most powerful shadowshaper of all and a vessel for all the shadows of Sierra's ancestors. However, this family history was hidden from Sierra by her mother and aunt Tia Rosa. Sierra discovers the shadowshapers of the community are under attack and being erased by Wick, the Columbia professor and anthropologist who has been trying to learn the shadowshapers' secrets to absorb their power for himself. To thwart Wick's evil scheme, Sierra and her friends, with the help of the librarian from Columbia University, unravel the mystery of Wick's takeover of the shadowshapers, and Sierra unlocks her potential as the new Lucera of the shadowshapers.

The reader learns throughout Sierra's quest that city life, while beautiful in many ways, is also fraught with complexity and conflict, which is identifiable in people's relationships with places within the city. Columbia University in Manhattan also serves as an important site where Sierra advances her quest. There, she is able to discover her family lineage outside of neighborhood lore. However, the relationship she has with the university and the knowledge she is able to glean by being there demonstrate the distinction between local knowledge and the academic trove of the Ivory tower. For Sierra, being on the Columbia campus positions her as "other," even though she is still in her home city: it was hard to believe the wide-open, ultramanicured campus of Columbia University was in the same city as Bed-Stuy. Sierra actually gasped when they walked through the front gates and stood surrounded by all those pillared temples of knowledge (44).

As an Ivy League school, Columbia represents the educated elite, the knowledge archive, and traditions of academia that, historically, have been complicit in the domination of black and brown peoples throughout the world (Smith 1999, 44). But also, it is typically the educated elite who contribute to the gentrification of city neighborhoods like Sierra's (National Geographic Society 2019). Historically, academics and black, brown, and lower-income communities have had complicated relationships. While, on one hand, research knowledge has been important for responding to local problems in communities of color and lower-income communities, on the other hand, much of the knowledge culled from local people gets stored away inside the walls of the university and never put to use for the benefit of the people whose knowledge was taken by researchers (Patel 2016, 12). We see this relationship in Sierra's encounter with the campus security guard as she enters the university's library: "'Where's your ID?' the security guard at the library entrance demanded. They were standing in an impossible marble foyer, and Sierra felt tiny, like a crumb in a giant pristine oven" (Older 2015, 45).

The security guard immediately identifies her as an outsider, and she feels her own insignificance in this enormous yet stifling space. When she finally does gain entrance and access to the books, she realizes that the stories of her ancestors have been locked away in this place and kept from her:

> Sierra had never seen so many books. *Economic Development in the Third World,* one title proclaimed loudly from a display table. *Studies in Puerto Rican Literature* said another. It'd never even occurred to her there was such a thing as Puerto Rican literature, let alone that it would be worthy of a thick volume in a Columbia University library. A smaller paperback was called *Debating Uncle Remus: An Anthology of Essays and Stories about the Historic Southern Folktales.* (Older 2015, 48)

Sierra is in high school and takes Advanced Placement classes. She is smart and educated, but we see here in this quote that she has also been removed from knowing her Puerto Rican heritage, which is an object of study in the walls of Columbia but not within her own schooling. Until this moment, Sierra is unaware of the rich literary history of her ancestors, a history which is kept alive by storyteller shadowshapers like Abuelo Lázaro. We also see the library as a built city space that simultaneously contains the history of Sierra's ancestors while excluding Sierra and other young people of color from accessing this history as a source of neighborhood capital. The Columbia University library, when contrasted with the Junklot, makes visible a paradox: in gentrifying neighborhoods, residents and their histories are cast off, crumpled scraps of paper, but in the library, they are neatly preserved, bound volumes pristinely locked away from the "disposability" of neighborhood life.

Although the Tower, the Junklot, and Columbia University are, perhaps, the starkest exemplars of the contradictions of the city, they are by no means the only examples. Older (2015) intersperses other urban scenery that contributes to the textured geography of city life that propels the plot. For instance, while much of the book is set in spaces dominated by concrete, we also see urban flora, as in the following example when Sierra first finds Robbie: "'He's right over there,' Tee said, 'by the mango tree or whatever that is, in that little dark garden area. Being creepy like always.' . . . Sierra made her way up the narrow path surrounded by an herb garden and some scrawny trees (15). It is notable that the foliage Older points out are not just trees or plants but also fruit trees and herbs, indicating sources of sustenance and healing around the city's inhabitants. Older also introduces the reader to Prospect Park. Spanning more than 500 acres in the center of Brooklyn, Prospect Park is filled with wildlife, water features, and cultural sites. This is also the location where Robbie teaches

Sierra how to channel and deploy her shadowshaping abilities: "They stood at a bend in the paved road that wound around Prospect Park, directly beneath a lamppost. Around her, the urban wilderness churned with cricket calls and the gentle swoosh of trees. Somewhere, a river flowed. The park was like a wooded city inside a much larger world of concrete" (133). Here, the reader is introduced to the natural habitats that coexist alongside man-made domiciles and contribute to the thriving of urban residents.

Still, too, we see how city landscapes bring history into the present and contrasting worldviews into contact. Older (2015) illustrates this phenomenon through Sierra's expressions of familiarity and/or fear in different locations. For instance, her journey through Flatbush and into an unfamiliar area of Brooklyn highlights how she is attuned to city geography, but certain parts of the landscape are disorienting because of their historical and social resonance:

> She had never been to Flatbush before, so she didn't even bother trying to figure out where she was heading. When you're lost in Brooklyn, the next corner store should only be a block or two in any direction, and they'd always be able to point the way to a nearby train. But somehow Sierra had stumbled into a quasi-suburban enclave of stand-alone houses, complete with front lawns and porch swings. It was creepy. The southern-style mansions glared out at her, making sure she had no designs on the untold secrets and treasures hoarded within. She turned corner after corner, panting as she hurtled through an endless night maze of creepy, tree-lined streets. (101)

The quasi-suburban, southern-style neighborhood emerges as a specter of the South, which conjures recollections of the nation's legacy of slavery and white supremacy. It is dark and sleeping but not dead, a threatening place that is unpredictable, unlike the lively Bed-Stuy neighborhood that is Sierra's home. These juxtapositions are a reminder that different lifeworlds coexist and are experienced in people's geographical connections even when they may seem worlds apart or long ago. Youth identity is also constituted in relation to the places where they dwell, as demonstrated in the next section.

Gentrification and Urban Youth Identity in *Shadowshaper*

Gentrification is a process of urban neighborhood change that occurs when college-educated, often white middle- and upper-middle-class populations begin relocating into working-class and lower-income neighborhoods that are typically populated by black and brown residents. As wealthier residents and businesses begin entering gentrifying neighborhoods, they bring new jobs, housing renovations, and various forms of capital and resources that can uplift the neighborhood. However, gentrification also increases the value of goods, services, and real estate, and it changes the demographics and culture of neighborhoods as well. These changes create challenges for the original residents who may begin to feel out of place, have a difficult time affording necessities, and may be pushed out of the neighborhood altogether (National Geographic Society 2019). Furthermore, gentrification fundamentally changes neighborhoods and creates cultural misalignments between those who lived in the neighborhood before gentrification began and the changing neighborhood itself and its new residents.

In the field of human geography, authors like Escobar (2001, 143) emphasize how culture is not simply carried within people's individual bodies; rather, culture "sits in places" and is enacted by and acts on people's identities through their connections with the lands they inhabit. In other words, environment both shapes and is shaped by people over generations. In urban spaces, just like any other spaces, residents have deeply rooted histories, and young people are both of and with their ancestors as they move through their daily lives in the present. Gentrification produces cultural clashes because the cultural connection between person and place is severed as the place is redesigned with the original residents still dwelling within it. Sierra's description of "The Takeover" is salient here. The original residents experience gentrification as a form of neocolonialism. As land is grabbed from those who live there, people who are indigenous to those lands are displaced and erased, like Papa Acadevo's fading mural.

Shadowshaper (Older 2015) makes this dynamic visible as the characters navigate their world. Sierra often notices the people of her community and reflects on the past in relation to the present as she moves from one location to the next while advancing in her quest. Take, for example, how Sierra observes the changing neighborhood while also observing the plight of the community and the development of the identities of young people within it:

> Bennie's corner of Brooklyn looked different every time Sierra passed through it. . . . A half block from where she stood, she'd skinned her knee playing hopscotch while juiced up on iceys and sugar drinks. Bennie's brother, Vincent, had been killed by the cops on the adjacent corner, just a few steps from his own front door. (82)

On one hand, we see childhood in the city during the summer. On the other hand, we see childhood stolen by the death of Bennie's brother at the hands of the police. Yet still, we see the neighborhood of the past disappearing even as Sierra's memories are very much alive.

Older (2015) illuminates the contradictory nature of what it means to be a brown woman living in a gentrifying place. Sierra has the sudden realization of her alienation even as she reminisces about her childhood in the exact place where her childhood played out:

> Now her best friend's neighborhood felt just like another planet. The place Sierra and Bennie used to get their hair done has turned into a fancy bakery of some kind, and yes, the coffee was good, but you couldn't get a cup for less than three dollars. Plus, every time Sierra went in, the hip, young white kid behind the counter gave her either the don't-cause-no-trouble look or the I-want-to-adopt-you look. The Takeover (as Bennie had dubbed it once) had been going on for a few years now, but tonight its pace seemed accelerated tenfold. Sierra couldn't find a single brown face on the block. It looked like a late-night frat party had just let out; she was getting funny stares from all sides—as if she was the out-of-place one, she thought. And then, sadly, she realized she was the out-of-place one. (83)

As the neighborhood is gentrifying, the places and people of the neighborhood are changing around Sierra, thereby changing her relationship with this urban space and changing her identity, too. Sierra ruminates over the fancy bakery and the three-dollar cup of coffee, highlighting the class distinction that is a marker of gentrification. She notices the looks she gets from the "young white kid behind the counter" who positions her, on one hand, as a threat (don't cause no trouble) and, on the other hand, as a pet (I want to adopt you). She is not the upper-class patron who is expected to be in the fancy coffee shop—she is either a criminal or a charity case. She finds herself a lone brown body in a sea of young white partygoers, which further draws the distinction between her deep community ties (getting her hair done with Bennie as a child) and the superficiality of the neighborhood as the location of a frat party for the newcomers.

In contrast to Sierra's feelings of displacement at the "late night frat party," Older deepens the connections between the neighborhood, history, and culture through the very bodies of the young protagonists themselves. For instance, Robbie, Sierra's love interest, carries images of his culture, ancestry, and city with him wherever he goes. Older writes, "Robbie was a tall Haitian kid with long locks who had shown up midyear with a goofy grin and wild drawings covering every surface of his clothes, his backpack, his desk" (9). Sierra identifies Robbie as a "walking mural"—which the reader comes to find is not an exaggeration—Robbie has pictures of ancestors tattooed in his skin. It is notable that Sierra falls in love with a boy who embodies his ancestors through his art, his actions, and his ink. Take, for instance, the following exchange when Sierra sees Robbie's tattoos for the first time.

> "That's a Taino, Sierra."
>
> "What? But you're Haitian. I thought Tainos were my peeps."
>
> "Nah, Haiti had 'em too. Has 'em. You know . . ."
>
> "I didn't know."
>
> The warrior gazed out across a teeming cityscape that crossed Robbie's abdomen and wrapped around his back. It was Brooklyn, Sierra realized, spotting the clock tower from downtown. Across from the Taino, a Zulu warrior-looking guy stood at attention, surrounded by the lights of Brooklyn. He held a massive shield in one hand and a spear in the other. . . . Just by Robbie's armpit, a little man in a three-pointed hat and a colonial jacket stared suspiciously off to the side, one hand gripping his sheathed sword.
>
> "Got a little French in you too, eh?" (127)

Even though he is Haitian and she is Puerto Rican, Robbie and Sierra share the common history of the Taino people who were conquered by Europeans. Both their ancestors migrated (or were displaced) and came to the United States and settled in Brooklyn. Now Sierra and Robbie are under the threat of displacement again, just as their ancestors were before them. But the tattoos remind Older's readers that Robbie's lineage consists of multiple warrior cultures, and those warriors are alive and with him in contemporary Brooklyn. In fact, Robbie explains that he gets his shadowshaping power from his ancestors, and when the young people go to battle leading into the climax of the novel, Robbie shadowshapes (brings to life) his tattoos. His ancestors magically emerge from his skin and fight against the ghosts that are attempting to destroy Sierra and her friends.

Sierra, too, finds her power to fight Wick and "the Sorrows" by drawing from her ancestors' strengths and struggles that are preserved in the geography of the city. In a culmination of events, Sierra and her friends rush to Coney Island as they decipher the riddle of a song Sierra's *abuela* sang to her as a child, "*come to the crossroads, to the crossroads come, where the powers converge and become one*" (188). There in the water, Sierra finds her *abuela* who is the Lucera, and abuela passes her gift to Sierra who is then able to channel the energy of all her ancestors to stop Wick and his army of undead throng haints (animated corpses):

> Sierra was Lucera, a fierce spiritual warrior like her abuela. She was stepping into her destiny. The spirits' intentions unified with hers. They were righteous, these spirits, and ferocious. They were not about to see their world destroyed at the hands of some old fool like Wick. No. They, Sierra and the spirits, would not be manipulated, dogged, oppressed. Not after so many years of struggle. . . . She raised her left hand. If there was no vessel for her to transmit the spirit into, she would be the vessel. (280)

As Sierra discovers her ability to channel all of the spirits through herself, to become one with her ancestry, she is able to emerge victorious in the fight against the ongoing threat of domination from Wick and the Takeover that he and the Tower represent.

Shaping Shadows: Resurrecting Urban Youth's Lineage of Struggle

When reading young adult fiction about urban spaces and urban youth, it is important to consider not only how young people are portrayed as embodying variations of "urbanness" but also how their identities are recursively intertwined with urban spaces and places because of their own history as well as the variegated histories of various peoples in the city. Popular images of urbanness link caricatures with particular geographical locations, simultaneously inscribing social meanings to both person and place. Fiction that presents urban young people as devoid of history and urban landscapes as devoid of life, culture, and lineage prevents readers from engaging with urban identities and urban landscapes in authentic ways that allow for a nuanced understanding of the historical roots of cities as contested spaces. Moreover, superficial renderings of city spaces and urban youth prevent readers from empathizing with urban young people as having deep ties to their neighborhoods. Throughout U.S. history, such artificial renderings of persons and places have propped up expansion and development projects that have destroyed, displaced, and erased indigenous and black and brown bodies from lands deemed valuable by white-settler populations (Tuck and Yang 2012, 28). Furthermore, stories like Older's underscore history as ongoing in the present, which forces an awareness of the ongoing imperialist project of "accumulation by dispossession" (Harvey 2009, 74), of which urban gentrification is just one recent iteration.

Such renderings stand in stark contrast to the interconnection between person and urban places represented in *Shadowshaper* (Older 2015). But even more so, texts like *Shadowshaper* show the plight of the city and its young people as dynamically intertwined. Older illuminates this in the final culmination of the text as Sierra embraces her shadowshaping power:

> She was the shimmering culmination of all her ancestors' strife, joyfulness, and struggle. She was a radiant child of spirit. She was a hundred different souls vibrating within a single living body. . . . She was on a horse in the rain forest, galloping toward freedom. She was alone in a cell, coming to terms for the four hundredth time with her imminent death and the deaths she'd dealt. She was in the rapture of

> love. She was ashamed. Her brain simmered with bursts of lilac, cigar smoke, sweat, the cringe of a missed opportunity, pangs of hunger. Most of all, though, she felt alive. The dead were so alive! (289–92)

Through their shared history, cities and urban youth infuse each other with vitality, vibrancy, and shared meaning. The city shares its people's stories through its murals, buildings, green spaces, bus routes, corner stores, and even junk lots. The shadows are everywhere, and there is much to learn from them if we choose to see them, shape them, and bring them to life.

Things to Think About

1. Kress and Patrissy highlight the relationship between the landscapes of cities and the identities of its inhabitants. What relationships do you see between the landscapes where you live, work, or attend school and your sense of self, as well as your connection to others?
2. The authors draw attention to how the interconnections between the history of city spaces and the history of city people are "written" on the built and natural environment. What evidence of this connection do you see in built and natural spaces you frequent?
3. Think of one of your favorite places to spend time in your hometown or someplace else that feels like home to you. What is it about this place that you feel drawn to? Why? Do you feel a sense of shared identity, culture, history, or something else? How does this self-awareness contribute to your thinking about the themes raised by the authors of this chapter?

Things to Explore

1. Bed-Stuy Arts Stroll. Murals. https://bedstuyartsstroll.com/murals/

2. Gregor, Alison. "Bedford-Stuyvesant: Diverse and Changing." *New York Times*, July 13, 2014. https://www.nytimes.com/2014/07/13/realestate/bedford-stuyvesant-diverse-and-changing.html.
3. Humans of New York. https://www.humansofnewyork.com/about
4. Nonko, Emily. "Living History: The Story Behind Bed-Stuy's Stunning Townhomes." *The Observer*, March 10, 2016. https://observer.com/2016/03/living-history-the-story-behind-bed-stuys-stunning-townhomes/.

References

Escobar, Arturo. 2001. "Culture Sits in Places: Reflections on Globalism and Subaltern Strategies of Localization." *Political Geography* 20(2): 139–74.

Harvey, David. 2009. "The 'New' Imperialism: Accumulation by Dispossession." *Socialist Register* 40(1): 63-87. https://socialistregister.com/index.php/srv/article/view/5811.

National Geographic Society. 2019. "Gentrification." In *National Geographic Education Resource Library*. www.nationalgeographic.org/encyclopedia/gentrification/.

Older, Daniel José. 2015. *Shadowshaper*. New York: Scholastic.

Patel, Leigh. 2016. *Decolonizing Educational Research: From Ownership to Answerability*. New York: Routledge.

Smith, Linda Tuhiwai. 1999. *Decolonizing Methodologies*. London: Zed Books.

Tuck, Eve, and K. Wayne Yang. 2012. "Decolonization Is Not a Metaphor." *Decolonization, Indigeneity, and Society* 1(1): 1–40.

CHAPTER FIVE

An Author's Perspective: Where I Can Plant the Seeds

Benjamin Alire Sáenz

I live the city on the U.S.–Mexico border. It is a city—El Paso, Texas—on the U.S. side of the border—and that is a very different thing than living in Juarez, which is also a city on the border—the same border. But Juarez is a city on the Mexican side of the border. That the two cities belong to different countries matters. But that the cities are only separated by a river that doesn't at all resemble a river creates a curious and clashing culture. These two countries are in love with each other. These two counties hate each other. The wars that they fight are often fought in my head, and they often embrace in my head. If you live here and have any compassion at all, then you will feel that somehow you belong to both cities and you will suffer from competing loyalties. Most people in this town suffer to a lesser or greater degree from such torn loyalties. Of course, there are also those people who, despite the fact that they live on the border, have no compassion at all for the people of Juarez, Mexico. None whatsoever. They, too, are a part of this community, although they have no wish to be a part of it.

This is where I live.

I have roots here. I know the history of the place, comprehend its political nuances. I understand and belong to its people and the kind of politics we have earned. I understand not only the loyalties but also the betrayals, and yet I do not quite understand why there has to be so much violence in Juarez and, in comparison, almost none in El Paso. Here, on the border, we understand that poverty is a violence created by the economic policies of both the United States and Mexico. And arising out of all this a culture arises that is neither Mexican nor American and that outsiders simply do not understand—because they do not want to understand. This border, this place, this city-in-two-cities is born of the collisions and embracings between two countries, two cultures, two linguistic traditions. Those collisions and embraces have brought into being cultural and linguistic practices that deconstruct and destroy the notion that a national identity has a kind of purity. There is an ignorance that Americans speak English and *only* English, and there is the blinder ignorance that other languages that enter the country represent a threat to who we are. Living on the border, it is obvious to me that Americans are often a scared people who are easily threatened. English is spoken all over Mexico and few people are afraid that Americans are trying to rob them of their Mexican identity. Why is it in the U.S., as powerful a nation if ever there were one, the reverse is true? As for me, I speak the languages of both countries, and I sometimes find myself thinking in both languages—but never at the same time. Like so many people here, I have mastered the art of code-switching and the art of creating new words that are neither Spanish nor English but are words, nonetheless. They are words that convey more accurately who we are because it is we who invented them and gave them life.

Where you live matters. And where you live shapes the way you live, the way you think, your vision of the world, the way you understand not only your own country, but the way you understand other countries as well. I think I understand the words *nation* and *nationalism* very differently than the majority of people do in this country in which I live because every day I am confronted with how constructed and unnatural national boundaries are. I understand that borders are necessary because nations must be able to control their own borders, but I also think that nations are not as necessary as we believe them to be. We might make the world a better place if we were to work toward creating a post-nationalist world. But that's not going to happen. We will cling to our borders and the idea of our nation, what it is, and what it stands for—even if it kills us. And it is killing us.

I like to believe that living here in the City of El Paso has made me a better man. Because I live in this particular city, I don't believe that Americans are superior to Mexicans. I don't believe that just because you were born in this country, it gives you any great claims to being superior. We talk about our freedoms and our way of life, and that we are a country of laws and as our great democratic system. We have come to believe that this country, by virtue of its political and legal institutions, and its democratic principles, has therefore produced a virtuous and superior people. But just as there are many Christians in this country who are Christians in name only, there are many Americans in this country who are Americans in name only. There are millions of Americans who don't believe in equality, and there are people who fly flags contrary to the flag they claim to honor. Americans are not a particularly virtuous people, not a particularly Christian people. In many ways, the Mexican people I am surrounded by, be they either Mexican Americans or Mexican nationals, are more virtuous than their American counterparts. As a whole, they embody a humility that is refreshing when compared to the sense of entitlement that runs rampant among the American populace, and their faith in God, their religious practices, and the values by which they live actually seem to have a relation to the message of the New Testament. Evangelical Christians seem not at all bothered by the fact that they support policies that are antithetical to the message found in the Bible they claim as sacred. I don't think that Americans consider Mexicans to be virtuous, and too many rely on the bigoted statements of President Trump to form their own opinion of an entire people. My experience of living on the border has given me a perspective on what it means to a decent human being, and I have not allowed the bias of national identities to cloud my ability to see people for what they are. National identities mean very little to me as a human being, as a writer, and as a poet. Because of my lifelong residence on the border, I stopped thinking that my U.S. citizenship contributed in any important way to my understanding of the human condition and the struggles of human beings as they grapple with questions of survival and live meaningful lives.

Because I live in a city that is on a border, I have come to see myself as a citizen of the world. As a young adult writer, I think of the children of the world as being *my* children in the sense that we, as adults, are charged with educating and caring for them. I am a gay man and I don't have any children. But that doesn't mean I don't consider the children of El Paso of Juarez to be my children. And that doesn't mean that the children of the world aren't my children either. All the children of the world *are* our children. Our allegiance to our nation can be destructive in that it can become a major impediment to seeing and understanding that we do, in fact, belong to each other—and it destroys the idea that every life matters. A child who was born in Moshi, Tanzania, is no less human than a child who was born in Lawrence, Kansas. Too great and strict an allegiance to our own country can become dangerously exclusive and promote the false idea that the life of a child that if is not of our nationality is none of our concern. We cannot absolve ourselves of the duty to care for and educate not only our children but also all the children of the world who are no less our children. Living in a city on the border has broadened my perspectives and has made me a more compassionate person. That, in turn, has made me a better human being. And that, in turn, has made me be a better writer.

Most of my work is set in El Paso and the U.S.–Mexico border. It is my privilege, my duty, and my responsibility to remind my readers that those of us who live here are a poor but dignified people whose generosity has something to teach to the rest of the nation. It should go without saying that we are human beings who deserve to be treated with respect. And I resent having to remind people of that rather obvious fact. Two of my most famous characters, Aristotle and Dante, are Mexican American boys—although I think my readers just see them as boys. But *it is* important they are Mexican American boys because my readers begin to see that difference does not mean that they are less human and less American than any of the other boys in America. It gets a little tiresome reading and hearing about what others say and think we are. We have our own voices, we can tell our own stories, we know how to tell them, and we can educate the rest of the world about who we are, and recount our struggles, our burdens, our poverty, and our ordinary lives that, in some ways, are lived quite differently from the lives of other Americans, but in so many other ways, we are all living lives that are not all that dissimilar. Most of us work hard, all of us trying to care for the people we love, juggling lives that are sometimes cluttered and chaotic, carrying the weight of our private hurts. We live on the edges of an America that often deliberately misunderstands us because it *refuses* to see who we are and refuses, too, to recognize our economic, cultural, political, artistic, educational, and intellectual contributions to our society. But my work stands as a reminder that is indeed an essential part of the life of this nation, and we are entitled to the rights extended to every other citizen—and many of us have been denied those rights illegally and for less-than-noble reasons.

Every writer has to know himself. How he comes to know himself is an important element in the journey of the self. I know who I am because I live in the City of El Paso. That is where the journey of the self began for me, and it is my great hope that that will also be the place where my journey ends. I have come to understand and love the people who live here, and I have come to understand that they are *my* people. Mine. That sense of belonging has made me realize that it is not so very important to view myself as a talented individual (whatever that is) but much more importantly as a member and a voice of my community. An art that is not an authentic part of the community that it seeks to represent will never be an art that matters—and it certainly will never be an art that is worthy of respect.

A writer has to have a sense that he is a part of something larger than himself. I belong to a city and to a people that have taught me to love and to speak and to be compassionate. I belong to a city that has taught me not be afraid of poverty because it is not something to be afraid of, it is not something to be ashamed of, and it certainly is not something that makes you less of a human being. Living here, on the border, has made me the writer that I am—and the man that I am. Every writer has to live and love and work and write from a place, a space. Every writer has to labor on a soil that he has earned the right to claim as his own, a soil where he can plant the seeds that spill from his mind and heart, and from his imagination and his curiosity. My poems and stories and novels all come from a garden named El Paso.

CHAPTER SIX

"Somewhere away from the Lights of the City": Unsettling the Normative Frameworks of Urban Space in Queer Young Adult Literature

Angel Daniel Matos

Representations of urban space in young adult (YA) narratives with queer[1] characters and themes are layered, complex, and, at times, challenging to examine. Although they often defy reductive and stereotypical approaches toward urban spatiality and geographies present in the broader fields of YA literature and popular culture, they simultaneously perpetuate common issues and misconceptions present in the queer literary "canon" and imagination. Ebony Elizabeth Thomas (2011), for instance, has argued that the term *urban* often has very specific uses and applications in YA literature, in that these texts describe such spaces as dangerous, poor, and, at times, violent. Thomas suggests that our popular consciousness often implements the language of "decay and the criminal justice system" when imagining urban spatiality, thus offering a biased and incomplete narrative of what urban dwelling means and what stories can ultimately be set in this space (17). Although this "gritty" perspective toward urban living is present in some queer YA narratives, such as Adam Silvera's (2015) *More Happy Than Not* and April Daniels's (2017) *Dreadnought*, many texts in this subfield can be approached as urban counternarratives, in that they frame these settings as utopic spaces where queer life can thrive and flourish. In queer narratives, urban spaces and, more specifically, cities are represented as loci for queer thought and experience—the ultimate destination for queer people to develop their sense of selves, come out, and be part of a large and vibrant community that rejects normative sexual and gender norms. But to what extent is this utopic narrative just as clichéd and formulaic as other approaches toward urban spatiality in the field of YA literature?

The understanding of urban spaces as advantageous to queer life and experience did not emerge from a vacuum and can be traced to social, cultural, and economic developments that took place in Western contexts in the nineteenth and twentieth centuries. Focusing on the case of New York City, which many people have approached as the heart of queer cultural life in the United States, George Chauncey ([1994] 2019) has pointed out that there are countless documented cases from the late 1800s onward of gay men moving to the city "because they were aware of homosexual interests they had to hide in their hometowns or because they were forced to flee when their secret was discovered" (135). The increasing perception of cities as aspirational destinations for queer men during this time could also be attributed to changes in urban economy and infrastructure. As Chauncey puts it, the city was a "logical" destination "for men intent on freeing themselves from the constraints of the family, because of its relatively cheap accommodations and the availability of commercial domestic services for which men traditionally would have depended on the unpaid household labor of women" (135). Others such as Phil Hubbard (2012) have suggested that the sheer size and scale of city spaces provided both a sense of liberation and protection for people who engage in nonnormative sexual practices, in that the city has historically "been regarded as a space of social and sexual liberation because of it is understood to offer anonymity and an escape from the more claustrophobic kinship and community relations of smaller towns and villages" (xiii). The spatial and social dimensions of the city largely assisted this location in becoming, to borrow the words of critic Scott Herring (2010), "an urban mecca to which rural-identified queers must assimilate" (14). The aforementioned historical developments (in addition to countless other sociocultural phenomena) helped to cement the notion of the cities as desirable and ideal locations in which queer life, desire, and community could thrive.

Historically, urban spaces have had quite a hold on the queer YA imagination. Countless YA novels with queer themes and characters are often set in large cities—and even when they are not, urban spaces still serve as imagined spaces that nonurban characters define themselves with or against. Some of the earliest and most groundbreaking queer YA texts were often set in urban geographies, and in many ways, these texts could be approached as a simultaneous exploration of queer desire and as a tour through the cities in which they are set. For instance, John Donovan's ([1969] 2010) *I'll Get There. It Better Be Worth the Trip,* arguably the first YA text with overt queer representation, is set in New York City. We observe a relationship developing between two teen boys as they travel through shops, Central Park, and the Museum of Natural History, and the text clearly articulates the affordances that city life can offer to its inhabitants. The novel's protagonist, Davy, further perpetuates this notion given that he was not raised in New York City and only begins to explore his queer desires within the narrative premises of city space. Davy's mother goes as far as to say that there is no place in the world such as New York City and continues to describe the location using the language of desire and possibility: "There's more of everything there. Got it? More of everything. Whatever you want, New York's got it" (28). Another classic queer YA text that bolstered the utopic possibilities of urban spaces was Nancy Garden's ([1982] 2007) *Annie on My Mind,* where teens Liza and Annie grow closer and develop an intense and supportive relationship while traveling through different areas of New York City, including park areas, rooftops, and museum exhibitions. The city provides Liza and Annie with the means to explore their relationship openly and publicly, providing them with a sense of anonymity that is stereotypically attributed to urban locations. At one point, they are even able to have a date at an Italian restaurant, where they are "separated by iron scrollwork partitions, so [they] had the illusion of privacy if not privacy itself" (108). Even classic queer YA texts that depart from the expectations of realism, such as Francesca Lia Block's ([1989] 2004) *Weetzie Bat,* take place in fictionalized versions of contemporary, real-world settings such as Los Angeles, further cementing the urban foundations of the field.

Although urban settings have been instrumental in the development of the queer YA imagination, we must be cautious, if not downright suspicious, of the utopic frameworks that are commonly projected onto these spaces—especially because many critics have pointed out the pitfalls of this thinking in queer contexts. Although Hubbard (2012) was upfront about the sexual possibilities that city spaces sometimes enable, he is quick to point out that representations of these possibilities are often exaggerated and misguided. He discloses how many queer people have "struggled to construct spaces of autonomy within the city," and many have had to "chisel out meeting spaces, exploiting the physical forms of metropolitan life" to challenge the fierce opposition that they have encountered in these contexts (18). Other scholars, such as Rae Rosenberg (2016), have discussed how racist ideologies informed the formation of gay urban spaces in the United States—ideologies that exclude the thoughts and experiences of queer people of color and people whose gender identities fall outside of the normative binaries held dear in Western contexts. Even more so, these racist logics and ideologies create hierarchies and binaries that pressure the queer freedoms that are commonly associated with cities. They "render White gay cisgender (cis) men more intelligible by, and more easily incorporated into, the state and mainstream national politics, and to have become reflected and secured as proper subjects in some gay urban spaces" (Rosenberg 2016, 3). Nonetheless, one of the greatest issues to be found in many representations of urban space in queer YA literature is that they often highlight and celebrate the affordances of city spaces by setting themselves in opposition to rural, nonurban settings—leading people to denote these latter contexts as "sexually conservative and even backward" (Hubbard 2012, xiv). In an ironic twist, queer YA literature that is set in the city frames this location as open, free, and emotionally nourishing, and it does so by taking the very elements used to stereotypically denote urban spaces in the YA field—such as violent, poor, and unsafe—and applying them toward the representation of rural spaces. In due course, it is precisely these ideologies and logics that have led to an uptick in metronormative values and attitudes.

In the study of queer spaces and geographies, *metronormativity* is a concept that was developed by queer theorists to describe the intense (and perhaps misguided) ties between urban spaces, queer communities, and queer desire. Even more so, the concept is used to describe the ways in which urban/city spaces are often framed as safer, more nourishing, and more conducive to the flourishing of queer life by casting nonurban spaces as threatening, lackluster, and lacking in queer comforts. Jack Halberstam (2005) has highlighted the mythical qualities of metronormativity, in that the "term reveals the conflation of 'urban' and 'visible' in many normalizing narratives of gay/lesbian subjectivities. Such narratives tell of closeted subjects who 'come out' into an urban setting, which in turn, supposedly allows for the full expression of the sexual self in relation to a community of other gays/lesbians/queers." (36) Metronormative ideologies not only highlight how rural and nonurban settings are devalued when it comes to the spatialization of contemporary Western queer identities, but they also further cement the faulty notion that rural spaces, unlike urban areas, are places of "suspicion, persecution, and secrecy" (37). Others, such as Herring (2010), have mobilized these critiques even further, claiming that metronormativity is often a major issue in the broader academic field, in that scholars often embrace populist forms of antiruralism (5). The tensions between urban and rural spaces, and the presence of metrocentric representations, are quite looming in the subfield of queer YA literature and culture.

In their examination of rural geographies in lesbian YA literature, Wendy Keys, Elizabeth Marshall, and Barbara Pini (2017) have argued that although some queer YA texts situated in rural settings highlight some of the positive elements of queer rural life, they still comply with metronormative ideals and uphold the belief that "queer identities can only be asserted and sustained through migration to the urban" (363). A prime example of this narrative would be Tawni Waters's (2014) *Beauty of the Broken*, which Keys, Marshall, and Pini critique for offering a scathing portrayal of rural queer life that elevates metrocentric ideologies: "The image of rurality it conveys is one of extraordinary violence, narrow mindedness and religious hatred.... The city, as represented by San Francisco, offers the only potential for a fulfilled queer life" (362–63). As mentioned before, even when a queer YA novel is set in a rural context, there is still a possibility that this text will still elevate metronormative ideals and fall into the trap of highlighting the pitfalls of rural life and the promises of life in the city. They accomplish this by either framing the city as a place that the queer protagonist wants or needs to move to, as in the case of *Beauty of the Broken*, and/or by framing rural spaces as dangerous, suffocating, and stifling for queer livability. Consider, for instance, Andrew Smith's (2014) dystopian text *Grasshopper Jungle*, which focuses on the experiences of queer teens who live in the fictional rural town of Ealing, Iowa. The novel's protagonist, Austin, has a lot of anxiety in expressing his queer desires toward his best friend, Robby—an anxiety that partially stems from living in a rural town where antiqueer attitudes and homophobia reign supreme. After he kisses Robby for the first time, he confesses that "If you ever want to get shot in Ealing, do *that* in someone's yard at night" (47), perpetuating the view of rural spaces as antithetical to queer desire and experiences. Although Austin's associations between his rural town and homophobic violence are not unwarranted, it is still important to note that queerness only achieves representation in this text through a spatial organizing logic that, as discussed by Julie Abraham (2009), presents "antigay violence as a product of rural locations" (275).

There is a major issue when it comes to the representation of geographical space in queer YA literature, one that leads to the continuation of hierarchical and problematic assumptions regarding understandings about queer living in urban and rural spaces. There is a broad, normative, and, at times, misguided perception of urban queers as more "advanced" and sophisticated in comparison to their rural counterparts—a perception that is informed by both spatial and temporal dimensions. As Herring (2010) suggests, there is a belief that "a metropolitan-identified queer will always be more dynamic, more cutting edge, more progressive, and more forward-looking than a rural-identified queer, who will always be more static, more backward, and more culturally backwater" (16). Beliefs such as these not only undercut the possibilities for queer identification, kinship, and community that can be found in rural and nonurban spaces, but in the case of queer YA literature, these beliefs can also lead readers to buy into the myth that there is only *one* ideal place and way to cultivate queer development: the city. While Thomas (2011) has rightfully highlighted the importance for "urban dwellers to recognize hope and possibility in the city" and for nonurban readers to "view cities as opportunities for new visions of empathy for others" (21), I argue that it is just as important for us to make sure that readers do not view certain geographies as the end-all and be-all for certain identities and life experiences. It is one thing to highlight the merits of urban life, but it is another thing to cast other geographies and spaces as lesser through this process of highlighting. This is precisely why it is important to keep intersectional frameworks in mind when conducting geographical analyses, for the identities that we embody affect the extent to which we feel a sense of belonging in a space.

Although urban locations are often framed as spaces of freedom and opportunity for queer characters, which characters are barred from these affordances due to the other identities that they embody? How about Aaron Soto in Silvera's (2015) *More Happy Than Not,* a New York City teen whose social class and ethnicity affect his ability to accept his attraction to other boys—thus leading him to undergo a medical procedure to suppress his queerness? How about the trans and genderqueer characters in Sassafras Lowrey's (2012) *Roving Pack,* who consistently struggle with homelessness, abuse, and violence while dwelling in Portland, Oregon?

I am not arguing that future queer YA novels should not be set in urban spaces, nor I am suggesting that *all* queer YA novels reinforce the urban/rural binary that creates palpable tensions in the queer YA imagination. However, I am pushing us to consider the complexity of urban spaces in the context of queer YA literature and to be mindful of how urban representation can make us engage in modes of thinking that are antithetical to the radical and emancipatory aims of many queer approaches. Moreover, we should continue developing an awareness of the ways in which texts reinforce or challenge metronormative ideologies regardless of the location in which they take place. A queer YA text can be set in an urban location without falling into the usual pattern of glorifying the city at the expense of tarnishing the perception of nonurban spaces. A text can be staged within the confines of a city and still highlight the ways in which other locations and settings can also be nourishing and invigorating for queer life and kinship. What is a strategy that we can implement in order to assess whether a queer YA text is representing a geographical location in a holistic and ethical fashion? One useful approach would be to determine whether the text implements double-voiced discourse when representing urban (and nonurban) spaces. YA critic Mike Cadden (2000) defines double-voiced discourse as the implementation of different frameworks, voices, and perspectives as "equal and provides alternative interpretations that offer, in their aggregate, no single and final answer for the reader. . . . Two or more ideological positions share the text without any one being in obvious control" (147). A YA novel that implements this discourse consciously offers readers multiple ways of reading, interpreting, and decoding the text through the presence of multiple viewpoints and ideological frameworks. In examinations of urban spatiality in YA literature, the existence of double-voiced discourse would entail not only a discussion of the affordances and drawbacks of queer urban life, but even more so, it would entail an exploration of the ways in which nonurban spaces provide opportunities for queer desire and kinship to proliferate. It would involve a celebration of the possibilities of queer urban life that is not contingent on the denunciation or depreciation of other ways of dwelling in the world.

I will now share a brief case study that focuses on the examination of urban and nonurban geographies in Benjamin Alire Sáenz's (2012) celebrated YA novel *Aristotle and Dante Discover the Secrets of the Universe*. I demonstrate how the novel deliberately implements double-voiced discourse to present readers with a holistic and ideologically complex understanding of the overlap between spatiality and queer potentiality. The presence of this double-voiced discourse, I argue, not only allows *Aristotle and Dante* to pressure metronormative concerns that have haunted the fields of queer YA literature and popular culture, but it also pushes us to be mindful of the fact that queer comforts and affordances can undoubtedly be found beyond the immediate confines of the urban. I selected this text not only because of its popularity and its focus on the experiences of queer Latinx teens growing up in the City of El Paso, Texas (a city that is not commonly represented in queer YA literature), but also because many of the text's events unfold in multiple urban and nonurban locations.

Case Study: *Aristotle and Dante Discover the Secrets of the Universe*

Aristotle and Dante's (Sáenz 2012) urban backdrop is upfront right from the first chapter of the novel, in which a radio DJ announces both the time and location in which the novel is set: "Wake up, El Paso! It's Monday, June fifteenth, 1987!" (6). The urban character of this novel, however, is sometimes difficult to detect, not only because of the novel's subtle implementation of spatiality but also because the novel is set in a city that is not as prevalent or as highly represented in YA literature when compared to locations such as New York and Los Angeles. As I have argued before, this novel is quite vague when it comes to its representation of space due not only to the lack of physical descriptions of the settings where the main characters dwell but also due to fact that this text focuses "more on its characters' psychological and mental development rather than their physical and environmental surroundings" (Matos 2019, 34). In spite of the novel's focus on its main characters' interiority, a close reading of the novel highlights the advantages that El Paso grants Ari and Dante as they grow closer to each other while exploring this urban space. For instance, they not only meet at a public pool present in the city but also spend time together while shopping at convenience stores, Mexican restaurants, and burger joints and riding "around on the bus all afternoon" (21). Living in El Paso provides Ari and Dante with the means to attain independent mobility, allowing them to privately and anonymously spend time together and learn about each other through their urban explorations, without adult or parental supervision—similar to the case of the characters in Garden's ([1982] 2017) *Annie on My Mind*.

The looming presence of this urban space, however, is pressured through the presence of another geography in which many of the novel's events unfold: the space of the desert. And it is precisely in this space that Ari begins to not only find out more about himself, but it is where he is also able to escape some of the pressures and normative pitfalls of urban living. Ari first visits the desert with Dante and his parents to stargaze. While peacefully resting under the blanket of the desert night sky, Ari not only laments the presence of light pollution in El Paso, but he places significant attention on the fact that he has found refuge "[s]omewhere away from the lights of the city" (Sáenz 2012, 41), a sentiment that Ari reiterates almost every time he returns to the desert to reflect and process both major and minor life events. This is one of the many moments in which Ari contrasts the possibilities or urban space with the comfort and belonging that he finds in the desert. Even more so, the sense of well-being that Ari feels in desert spaces when contrasted with the space of the city is remarkable—a comfort that becomes increasingly necessary as Ari struggles to come to grips with his sexuality and identity. Part of this has to do with the fact that the desert provides Ari with a break from the pressures and expectations that he must grapple with as a Latinx teen, but we must also be mindful of the sociocultural burdens present within the geography that Ari inhabits. Emma Pérez (2012) has discussed the pressures that queer people have had to deal with while growing up in El Paso, suggesting that many of the queer folx inhabiting this city must "negotiate a severely racist and heteronormative colonial space that attempts to negate their lived experiences" (206). Although Ari repeatedly ventures out into the desert to escape the city lights, we cannot help but wonder what else Ari might be escaping from.

El Paso's urban character is not only pressured through the presence of desert spaces in the novel, but it is also pressured through the representation of another metropolis later on in the text: Chicago. Dante's father receives a visiting professorship at an institution in this midwestern city, and the whole family lives in Chicago for about a year as Dante and Ari continue to develop their relationship through written correspondence. Chicago is an urban location with a rich and vibrant queer history, and even more so, it is a city that is—at least stereotypically—viewed as more open and accepting of nonnormative sexualities and gender identities when compared to places such as El Paso. While in Chicago, Dante not only gets access to more freedoms and experiences that he did not have access to in El Paso, but he also begins to be more open about his sexuality and his queerness during this temporary visit—which situates Dante's development pretty neatly within a metronormative narrative. Dante starts experimenting with alcohol, drugs, and kissing with girls (Sáenz 2017, 175–76), and it is during these experimentations that he begins the coming-out process. In a letter that he writes to Ari, Dante admits to thinking about boys when kissing girls, and he also expresses exhaustion from hanging out in Chicago: "*even though it's been a real trip hanging out with privileged Chicago kids who can afford lots of beer and liquor and pot, they're really not all that interesting. Not to me anyway. I want to go back home*" (226, emphasis in original). The moments in which Dante discusses his experiences in Chicago are crucial. On one hand, the presence of multiple urban locations in the text unsettles the tendency of creating a monolithic narrative of what queer urban life entails and demonstrates that cities can vary in terms of resources, geographies, and access to queer solaces. On the other hand, it also shows how these comforts and affordances are insufficient for Dante and how they are unable to provide him with a complete sense of fulfillment and validation seen in other queer narratives set in large cities. In spite of Dante's denunciation of Chicago, it is undeniable to see the effect that living in this city had on his overall demeanor, attitude, and acceptance of his queerness. Dante begins to talk more openly about his sexuality, contemplates the possibility that he will marry a boy in the future, and even starts dating Daniel, one of his coworkers.

Dante's open embrace of his queerness contrasts significantly with Ari's journey of self-acceptance not only because the latter has difficulties expressing his emotions but also because he feels shame at admitting his love for Dante. Whereas Dante's experiences in the space of the city provide him with the means to open up and explore his emerging queerness, Ari's queerness and desire for Dante flourish instead in the space of the desert. It is in the space of the desert where the two friends discuss Dante's fears of coming out to his parents. It is in the desert where Ari begins to express himself in ways that he has not before, and he starts to convey emotions such as anger, shame, and pain—feelings he desperately tried to contain within. It is in this space where he breaks down and starts to show physical and emotional vulnerability to Dante, especially as they sit out in the desert while Ari processes an argument that he had with his parents: "I don't know why I was yelling. The yelling turned into sobs. I fell into Dante's arms and cried. He held me and didn't say a word" (Sáenz 2017, 261). Unsurprisingly, the desert also stages the novel's conclusion, where Ari finally comes out to Dante and admits his feelings toward him. Note, in particular, how the language of freedom is used to describe the aftermath of this coming out moment in the desert: "As Dante and I lay on our backs in the bed of my pickup and gazed out at the summer stars, I was free. Imagine that. Aristotle Mendoza, a free man. I wasn't afraid anymore" (359). I find this moment quite striking, especially since the desert is used to frame and color our perception of this moment of queer kinship and desire.

Whereas it may be easy to approach deserts as spaces of lifelessness, emptiness, and death, *Aristotle and Dante* (Sáenz 2017) instead approaches this space as one of freedom, hybridity, and joy—which aligns this novel closely with how many Latinx and Chicanx texts frame this space. Ralph J. Poole (2016), for instance, argues that the desert in this novel is a type of borderlands. The novel frames deserts as a space that "encapsulates and transcends his hybrid Chicano identity," and even more so, it becomes a "multifarious ecotone, where differing cultures, sexualities, and temperaments meet" and where future social relationships are mapped (127). Along these lines, Herring (2010) has pointed out the usefulness of "rural stylistics" in challenging metronormative ideals and values, which can broadly be described as "stereotypically ruralizing stylistics of rusticity, stylessness, unfashionability, anti-urbanity, backwardness, anti-sophistication, and crudity" (22). *Aristotle and Dante*'s implementation of desert spaces, in many ways, is emblematic of these rustic, antiurban stylistics due not only to the lack of the amenities, infrastructure, and sociocultural elements present in urban spaces but, even more so, due to the cultural associations of death, lifelessness, and extremity associated with this environmental space. Drawing from Chicanx literary and spatial traditions and discourse on borderlands, the novel demonstrates how the desert is capable of being a backdrop for queer desire and demonstrates how queer kinship and futurity can be indeed be found, identified, and sustained somewhere away from the city lights.

I do not want to argue that *Aristotle and Dante* simply critiques the metronormative ideals associated with queer city life, or that the novel highlights the queer possibilities found in nonurban spaces at the expense of the urban. But rather, I suggest that the novel consciously implements double-voiced discourse when representing geographical locations—a discourse that provides readers with different interpretative possibilities when it comes to the representation of queer teens and the spaces that they dwell in. Even though the novel is very much urban in its setting and sensibilities, I find the novel to be refreshing in its representation of the queer affordances that can (or cannot) be found within urban contexts. Sáenz's (2017) novel highlights the ways in which urban spaces facilitate the exploration of queer desire and relationality, but it also reminds us that these spaces are not always conducive to the sensibilities, desires, cultures, or journeys of every queer person. The novel not only shows different cities with different queer potentialities, but it also shows the ways in which queerness and kinship can be discovered and nourished in nonurban locations.

Whereas many queer YA novels end up creating a hierarchy between urban and nonurban space and perpetuate metronormative ideologies in the process, *Aristotle and Dante* (Sáenz 2017) engages in a leveling project of sorts, putting into practice the concept of the ecotone that is overtly discussed in the text: "It's the terrain where two different ecosystems meet. In an ecotone, the landscape will contain elements of the two different ecosystems. It's like a natural borderlands" (238). Ari and Dante develop queerly not through prioritizing the urban over the nonurban but by dwelling in the ecotone between these spaces. Rather than augmenting the ideological tensions found in representations of queer urban life and further creating a wedge between the city and nonurban spaces, this text pushes us to dismantle these tensions and divides. And it does so through its ideological complexity, in that it offers multiple and competing discourses of the limits and affordances of urban and nonurban settings vis-à-vis queer kinship and desire.

Things to Think About

As you continue to engage in examinations of urban space in queer YA literature, it is important to recall the ways in which the text's setting and spatiality affects the dynamics and ideologies represented in it. Here is a list of discussion questions that might spark important and useful thinking as you examine the urban geographies of queer YA literature:

1. Describe how a queer character approaches the space of the city. Does the character view urban locations as spaces full of potential, promise, and possibility? Do they view cities as suffocating, restricting, and/or dangerous spaces? How else do they describe these locations? To what extent does the queer character's other identities (such as race, ethnicity, social class, disability) affect how they approach and relate to city spaces?
2. How important is the text's setting when it comes to the emotional, psychological, intellectual, and physical development of its queer character(s)? Does the novel's setting have major effects or influences on the character's well-being, the acceptance of their sexuality and/or gender identity, and their relationships with other characters?
3. To what extent does the queer YA novel implement a double-voiced discourse when representing urban spaces and geographies? In other words, does the novel present multiple, and perhaps competing, perspectives and interpretations toward the urban spaces it represents? Is the representation of a city limited to the perspective of one character, or do we get the perspectives of multiple characters throughout the text? Does the text ultimately challenge or reinforce metronormative perspectives?

Things to Explore

For those interested in queer YA literature that contains ideologically complex and layered representations of (or perspectives toward) cities/urban spaces, please check out the following young adult novels:

1. **Danforth, Emily M. *The Miseducation of Cameron Post.* New York: Balzer + Bray, 2012.** Although New York City, San Francisco, and Los Angeles are some of the most commonly represented cities in queer YA literature, this narrative is set in late 1980s' Miles City, Montana. Although set in a city, this novel pressures and unsettles many of the utopic potentialities associated with urban queer life by focusing on a lesbian teen being raised by her conservative, religious aunt after the death of her parents.
2. **Rivera, Gabby. *Juliet Takes a Breath.* New York: Riverdale Avenue Books, 2016.** This novel can enrichen our understanding of queer adolescent life in urban spaces through its representation of two different cities. Queer Latinx protagonist, Juliet, travels from the Bronx, New York to Portland, Oregon, to work as an intern for a queer feminist author. Although representations of city spaces can be universalizing and monolithic, this text offers readers two different cities with vastly different social, cultural, geographic, and economic realities. This layered representation of queer city life is further enriched through the novel's examination of intersectional identity and oppression, showing readers how different geographical contexts give rise to diverging ideological frameworks regardless of their urban character.
3. **Silvera, Adam. *They Both Die at the End.* New York: HarperCollins, 2017.** Told from the perspectives of various characters and taking place in a speculative future in which people receive a phone notification on the day that they are going to die, this novel implements a double-voiced discourse to represent the city as both a site of queer possibility and as a place of danger

and decay. In a sense, the novel can be approached as a one-day tour of a city, offering a more holistic and ideologically rich representation of the overlap between queer adolescent life and city spaces.

Notes

1. As I discuss in other research projects that I've developed, I use the term queer as a consciously broad and inclusive umbrella term when referring to nonheterosexual and noncisgender people, cultures, communities, and experiences. I do this to avoid the issues of inclusion and exclusion present in the use of terms such as LGBTQ+ and 2SLGBTQIA, among others. In many ways, my use of this term meshes with Michael Warner's (1999) definition, which he describes as a flexible way of approaching the "many ways people can find themselves at odds with straight culture" (38).

References

Abraham, Julie. 2009. *Metropolitan Lovers: The Homosexuality of Cities*. Minneapolis: University of Minnesota Press.

Block, Francesca Lia. (1989) 2004. *Weetzie Bat*. New York: HarperTeen.

Cadden, Mike. 2000. "The Irony of Narration in the Young Adult Novel." *Children's Literature Quarterly* 25(3): 146–54.

Chauncey, George. (1994) 2019. *Gay New York: Gender, Urban Culture, and the Making of the Gay Male World, 1890–1940*. 2nd ed. New York: Basic Books.

Daniels, April. 2017. *Dreadnought*. New York: Diversion.

Donovan, John. (1969) 2010. *I'll Get There. It Better Be Worth the Trip*. 40th anniversary ed. Woodbury, MN: Flux.

Garden, Nancy. (1982) 2007. *Annie on My Mind*. New York: Square Fish.

Halberstam, Jack (published as Halberstam, Judith). 2005. *In a Queer Time and Place: Transgender Bodies, Subcultural Lives*. New York: New York University Press.

Herring, Scott. 2010. *Another Country: Queer Anti-Urbanism*. New York: New York University Press.

Hubbard, Phil. 2012. *Cities and Sexualities*. New York: Routledge.

Keys, Wendy, Elizabeth Marshall, and Barbara Pini. 2017. "Representations of Rural Lesbian Lives in Young Adult Fiction." *Discourse: Studies in the Cultural Politics of Education* 38(3): 354–64.

Lowrey, Sassafras. 2012. *Roving Pack*. Brooklyn, NY: Pomo Freakshow.

Matos, Angel Daniel. 2019. "A Narrative of a Future Past: Historical Authenticity, Ethics, and Queer Latinx Futurity in *Aristotle and Dante Discover the Secrets of the Universe*." *Children's Literature* 47(1): 30–56.

Pérez, Emma. 2012. "Decolonial Border Queers: Case Studies of Chicana/o Lesbians, Gay Men, and Transgender Folks in El Paso/Juárez." In *Performing the US Latina and Latino Borderlands*, edited by Arturo J. Aldama, Chela Sandoval, and Peter J. García, 192–211. Bloomington: Indiana University Press.

Poole, Ralph J. 2016. "Boys Kissing in the Desert: Benjamin Alire Sáenz's *Aristotle and Dante Discover the Secrets of the Universe*." *The Explicator* 74(2): 125–28.

Rosenberg, Rae. 2016. "The Whiteness of Gay Urban Belonging: Criminalizing LGBTQ Youth of Color in Queer Spaces of Care." *Urban Geography*. Published ahead of print, September 29. https://doi.org/10.1080/02723638.2016.1239498.

Sáenz, Benjamin Alire. 2012. *Aristotle and Dante Discover the Secrets of the Universe*. New York: Simon and Schuster Books for Young Readers.

Silvera, Adam. 2015. *More Happy Than Not*. New York: Soho Teen, 2015.

Smith, Andrew. 2014. *Grasshopper Jungle*. New York: Dutton.

Thomas, Ebony Elizabeth. 2011. "Landscapes of City and Self: Place and Identity in Urban Young Adult Literature." *The ALAN Review* 38(2): 13–22.

Warner, Michael. 1999. *The Trouble with Normal*. Cambridge, MA: Harvard University Press.

Waters, Tawni. 2014. *Beauty of the Broken*. New York: Simon Pulse.

CHAPTER SEVEN

Anti-Urbanism in Willa Cather's Mythical West

Melinda Knight

Willa Cather once said in an interview that "the farmer's wife who raises a large family and cooks for them and makes their clothes and keeps house and on the side runs a truck garden and a chicken farm and a canning establishment, and thoroughly enjoys doing it well, contributes more to art than all the culture clubs" (Hinman 1921). This marvelous housewife, although today we might see her more as an agricultural manager, with her "appreciation of the beautiful bodies of her children, of the order and harmony of her kitchen, of the real creative joy of all her activities," is, in Cather's view, a "great artist" (Hinman 1921). Cather thus glorifies pioneer life and contributes to the archetype of the homesteader, even though she herself was never a farmer, a housewife, a mother, or, after her childhood in Virginia and Nebraska, a resident of rural America. Cather's life was a complicated effort to be recognized as a serious artist for her journalism, for her fiction, and for her poetry. Her life thus contradicts what has been most admired about her work, the everyday struggles of ordinary people living on the Great Plains. In this chapter, I show how Cather's narratives both reinforced a mythic and anti-urban view of the American West while simultaneously using strategies of the financial industry most identified with urban life.

I look closely at perhaps her best-known novel, whose name speaks for itself, *O Pioneers!* ([1913] 2008).

Cather was born 1873 in Virginia and given the name Wilella, which she later changed to Willa. Her family moved nine years later to central Nebraska, where her father tried and failed at farming. The family subsequently relocated to Red Cloud, where her father started a farm loan and insurance business. During her youth, she experimented with cross-dressing and gave herself the name William Cather M.D., the latter an expression of an early desire to become a surgeon, an occupation generally reserved for men. After graduating from the University of Nebraska in 1896, she worked for a time for the *Nebraska Home Journal* and then moved to Pittsburgh and continued working as a journalist. At the age of thirty-three, she moved to New York City, where she lived until her death.

Cather has long presented problems of interpretation for her critics and fans. In the 1920s, she was praised by reviewers and also achieved popular success. She won the Pulitzer Prize for the novel in 1923 for *One of Ours*, only the second woman to have done so after Edith Wharton won for *The Age of Innocence* in 1921. She was financially rewarded as well. When her 1927 novel *Death Comes for the Archbishop* was ready for distribution, she asked her publisher for an increase in royalties and received it, telling Alfred Knopf that his son would be paying the book's royalties to her niece (Knopf 1975, 210).

Cather then suffered the fate of so many American women writers, as she became considered a minor, not major, writer, perhaps of more interest to the local color or regionalist schools of literature. The influential editor Clifton Fadiman (1932) was a typical proponent of this view, as he suggests that Cather's emphasis on the historical past would "permanently transport her to regions where minor works of art may be created, but major ones never" (563). Fadiman, who was head of the *New Yorker*'s book review section from 1933 to 1943 and later a Book-of-the-Month Club judge, undoubtedly contributed to the decline in Cather's reputation, what Sharon O'Brien (1988) has termed a "decanonization." In this process, certain works are demoted from the canon, the works considered greatest and most important, and others are elevated. I remember well my experiences in English classes in college, for we were never assigned works by Cather, and the only woman writer we read was Emily Dickinson. Fortunately, the second-wave feminist movement, which began in the 1960s, also produced transformations in how literature was read and valued, and now many women writers previously ignored, including Willa Cather, are taught all across the curriculum in elementary, middle schools, high schools, and colleges and universities.

The current revival of interest in Cather has, nevertheless, been fraught with contradictions. Some still celebrate her as a native of Nebraska and faithful chronicler of pioneer life. More recently, feminist critics have focused on her lesbianism and made her a feminist icon. Her life is revered in Red Cloud, Nebraska, the site of many of her novels and stories under various names, and yet the Willa Cather Foundation (n.d.), which is dedicated to preserving the "the historical settings and archival material associated with her life and work," does not mention anything about her sexual orientation. In addition to organizing conferences and seminars and publishing the *Willa Cather Review*, the foundation is responsible for restoring and conserving the 612-acre Willa Cather Memorial Prairie. The prairie plays a leading role in the three novels of her "prairie trilogy"—*O Pioneers!* ([1913] 2008), *The Song of the Lark* ([1915] 2008), and *My Ántonia* (1918). Any of these novels would be a good choice for a course on young adult literature, although my focus will be on the first.

Cather's prairie trilogy illustrates the enduring myth of the frontier in American culture, which itself is an anti-urban concept. The historian Richard Slotkin (1973) calls the frontier as a way to see America as a "wide-open land of unlimited opportunity for the strong, ambitious, self-reliant individual to thrust his way to the top" (5). This "wide-open land" offers an alternative to Thomas Jefferson's (1800) abhorrence of the city as "pestilential to the morals, the health and the liberties of man." Frederick Jackson Turner ([1920] 2007), in his famous address to the American Historical Association at the World's Columbian Exhibition in 1893, lamented what the closing of the frontier, as reported by the 1890 U.S. Census, would mean for the future of democracy in America. What became known as the Turner Thesis contributed to the mythic status of the frontier and provided a justification for westward expansion. Slotkin (1973) further defines myth "as a set of narratives that acquire through specifiable historical action a significant ideological charge" (19). Narratives of life on the frontier, whether by pioneers or by cowboys, have long appeared prominently in many of the arts, especially fiction, television, shows, and even video games such as The Oregon Trail. Even today, people often invoke the notion of "pioneering spirit" to define what has been regarded as exceptional about America.

Related to the frontier myth is the safety-valve theory of open space, the notion that unemployment in urban areas in the East could be "relieved" by opening up free land in the West. Hence, the Homestead Act of 1862 provided 160 acres to anyone willing to farm the land, build a home, and make improvements over a period of five years, a process known as "proving up," at which point the property title would revert to the homesteader. Some 270 million acres, or about 10 percent of the total land of the United States, were given away under the Homestead Act, which was subsequently revised several times until it was repealed for all but Alaska in 1976. The Homestead Act represented the first giveaway of land in the public domain. A claimant needed to be a U.S. citizen, or to have expressed the intention to become one, and had to certify never bearing arms against the government, a provision made to exclude fighters for the Confederacy. A total filing fee of $18, plus final proof of proving up, was all that was required. Nebraska, the site of many of Cather's novels, distributed the most land of all the states, and all three novels in the prairie trilogy focus on pioneer families who arrived as homesteaders.

The title of *O Pioneers!* consciously alludes to Walt Whitman's "Pioneers! O Pioneers!"—a poem that, like the novel, extols the pioneering spirit. The novel received many positive reviews. The *New York Times Book Review* noted how large looms "the earth, the land, patient and bountiful source of all things" ("Hundred" 1913, R664). The *Times,* which selected the novel as one of the year's best books, also saw it as a "story of the final conquest of Nebraska's untamed soil." "Conquest" is an interesting choice of words here, for many historians have reacted to the Turner Thesis by seeing expansion in the west as violence and imperialism as opposed to growth and development. Patricia Limerick (1987), for example, describes the "history of the West" as a "study of a place undergoing conquest and never fully escaping its consequences" (26).

Cather places her poem "Prairie Spring" as an epigraph to the novel and immediately introduces images of the land: "flat," "rich and sombre," with "miles of fresh-plowed soil." The poem also speaks to the stories that will soon be told in the novel: "youth, flaming like the wild rose," "unsupportable sweetness," and "earthiness." The novel is not one story but two. Carl Linstrum and Alexandra

Bergson are at the center of one story, which ends well, and her brother Emil and Marie Shabata are in the other and meet a tragic end.

The novel begins with a nostalgic view of Red Cloud, Nebraska, here called Hanover:

> One January day, thirty years ago, the little town of Hanover, anchored on a windy Nebraska tableland, was trying not to be blown away. . . . The dwelling houses were set about haphazard on the tough prairie sod; some of them looked as if they had been moved in overnight, and others as if they were straying off by themselves, headed straight for the open plain. None of them had any appearance of permanence, and the howling wind blew under them as well as over them. (Cather [1913] 2008)

This opening suggests the struggle of homesteaders to make it, in this case a family of Swedish immigrants, and yet it is significant that the story opens in town, not on the farm. Not often recognized is how many people were living in cities in what we call the West, even during the time this novel is historically set. We first meet Alexandra Bergson when she helps rescue her younger brother Emil's kitten—a rescue carried out by Carl Linstrum, who is to be her lifelong friend and possible companion. Both Alexandra and Carl have been uprooted from their homes in Europe and transported to the prairie of Nebraska. Alexandra is described as a "strong girl," who walked rapidly and resolutely as if she knew exactly where she was going and what she was going to do next (1).

The novel contains five separate sections, "Wild Land," "Neighboring Fields," "Winter Memories," "The Mulberry Tree," and "Alexandra" and spans a total of some seventeen years from about 1883, when the story begins. Throughout appear images of the land, which many commentators view as a character in its own right. But I would like to focus on a more sinister aspect of the focus on land, the way it functions as a commodity and financial asset. For that we need to return to the beginning of the novel.

After the opening scene in Hanover, we learn that Alexandra's father, John Bergson, is dying and that he is passing the mantle of head of the household to Alexandra rather than to her brothers. She thus inherits the job of managing both the family household and the farm. For several years after her father's death, Alexandra and her family prosper, but then bad times come with the drought, and all their crops are ruined. Here we have a familiar story of struggle against adversity and what untamed nature can do. Alexandra, however, refuses to be discouraged, and she decides to "drive down to the river country and spend a few days looking over what they've got down there." She and Emil, during a five-day trip, travel all over the valley and talk "to the men about their crops and to the women about their poultry." She spends one entire day with a farmer who has learned more about agriculture from school and is "experimenting with a new kind of clover hay." After looking at the land that everyone else thinks is more desirable, she decides to hold on to the "high land," the area known as the Divide, where they live now. On the way home, she has an epiphany about the land:

> For the first time, perhaps, since that land emerged from the waters of geologic ages, a human face was set toward it with love and yearning. It seemed beautiful to her, rich and strong and glorious. Her eyes drank in the breadth of it, until her tears blinded her. Then the Genius of the Divide, the great, free spirit which breathes across it, must have bent lower than it ever bent to a human will before.

This passage has often been interpreted as an example of the land as character or Alexandra as an earth mother or corn goddess, and my students tend to agree with this approach. But it is useful to separate what characters or narrators say they are doing from what they actually do. In other words, as the saying goes, actions speak louder than words. In this case, Alexandra has decided that the best course of action for her and her family is to engage in land speculation. As she explains to her brothers,

> [t]he rich men down there own all the best land, and they are buying all they can get. The thing to do is to sell our cattle and what little old corn we have, and buy the Linstrum place. Then the next thing to do is to take out two loans on our half-sections, and buy Peter Crow's place; raise every dollar we can, and buy every acre we can.

When her brothers protest about assuming further mortgages, she has ready explanations:

> We borrow the money for six years. Well, with the money we buy a half-section from Linstrum and a half from Crow, and a quarter from Struble, maybe. That will give us upwards of fourteen hundred acres, won't it. You won't have to pay off your land mortgages for six years. By that time, any of this land will be worth thirty dollars an acre—it will be worth fifty, but we'll say thirty; then you can sell a garden patch anywhere, and pay off a debt of sixteen hundred dollars. It's not the principal I'm worried about, it's the interest and taxes. We'll have to strain to meet the payments. But as sure as we're sitting here to-night, we can sit down here ten years from now independent landowners, not struggling farmers any longer.

What Alexandra has learned already, by observing the rich property owners down near the river, is that the monetary value of land, not its agricultural output, will determine who succeeds and achieves what we call the American Dream. All that remains is to hold tight.

She was right, for the drought finally ends and she becomes rich, not by farming the land herself as a single woman homesteader but by speculating and acquiring as much property on the margin as possible. The novel abruptly shifts to a point thirteen years later, and "the Divide is now thickly populated" and the "rich soil yields heavy harvests." Curiously, Alexandra is the only successful person portrayed in the novel. She is surrounded by a culture of her own making—the result of her enormous talents as a businesswoman. The practices most often associated with urban life and, especially, in financial centers, real estate development and speculation, are imposed on the frontier in a mythical west.

At first glance, it would seem that Alexandra's newfound prosperity proves the success of the Homestead Act. But she did not prove up her own land; she instead bought failing properties at rock-bottom prices. Historians now consider the Homestead Act to be largely a failure. Of some two million claims filed, only 40 percent were successful; that means 60 percent of those who began the process never completed it. Within those 40 percent who did, many were from the same family. There are numerous reasons for the lack of success. The soil was of poor quality in many places, the new farmers did not know much about farming, and natural disasters were a regular occurrence.

Homesteaders also had to compete with land speculators, who could buy land immediately at $1.25 an acre without doing any proving up. In the ten years preceding passage of the Homestead Act, almost 128 million acres of land were granted to the railroads, in many cases land that was more productive for farming. When land near the tracks opened up, the prices soared, far beyond the reach of prospective homesteaders. But the most important reason for the failure of homesteading was the fact that a plot of 160 acres with no irrigation was simply not enough to support farming on such a small scale in the Great Plains. My own family was one such example. My great-grandmother and her children traveled by covered wagon in 1878 from Mt. Clemens, Michigan, to western Kansas near what is now Ness City, some 180 miles southwest of Red Cloud. After building a sod house and struggling for five years in the drought at that time, they gave up and returned to the urban center of Kansas City.

Alexandra does not need to succeed as a homesteader, for she demonstrates the keen eye of a bargain shopper. The values she sees in other properties, however, does not increase by themselves, even though she claims "the land did it" and "had its little joke": "It pretended to be poor because nobody knew how to work it right; and then, all at once, it worked itself." No, the land is not valuable in itself, despite all the powerful images. The land she acquires is valuable because others have already proved up and shown it is fertile. The land is valuable because someone, Alexandra, has learned how to exploit it. The novel thus ruptures another agrarian myth, that of the solo subsistence farmer. By the end of the nineteenth century, large farms were already replacing smaller ones, as farming increasingly became industrialized and mechanized.

In addition to situating a literary text in the social and historical context, I have always found what is left out to be a useful category of analysis. There are two striking absences in *O Pioneers!*—one related to the action of the story and the other to the historical setting and particularly its people. Some thirteen years have elapsed between the end of "Wild Land," when Alexandra decides to buy up her neighbors' property, and the opening of the second part of the novel, "Neighboring Fields." During this time, Alexandra has greatly increased the value of her holdings, but how? It all seems magical, as if the land simply existed with no labor. Who farmed it? In the preceding chapter, she assures her brothers that they will not have to work the land:

> You poor boy, you won't have to work it. The men in town who are buying up other people's land don't try to farm it. They are the men to watch, in a new country. Let's try to do like the shrewd ones, and not like these stupid fellows. I don't want you boys always to have to work like this. I want you to be independent, and Emil to go to school.

Here, again, she shows her financial shrewdness by understanding that paying other laborers will be more lucrative than having her own family do the work. The farm labor becomes another commodity to be bought and sold. We do not find out much if any about what happened, although we know that she presides over the meal table of her workers.

The second notable absence is any mention whatsoever of Native Americans, whose land has been appropriated for all the pioneers. The word *Indian* appears only twice: once when a character suggests that a baby must have a squaw ancestor, for he looks "exactly like the Indian babies," and then when Alexandra asks Carl if his planned trip to Alaska is to "paint the Indians." Red Cloud, which is Hanover in the novel, was named for the great chief of the Oglala Lakota tribe. The Willa Cather National Center (n.d.) reports that Red Cloud "is said to be the most famous little town in America" but goes on to say that although it was named for the Lakota chief, "there is no evidence of Sioux having been in this area." Red Cloud, whose name in Lakota is Mahˇpíya Lúta, was born in North Platte, Nebraska. Native Americans do appear in some of Cather's other works, but I find their absence striking in *O Pioneers!*

At the end of the novel, Alexandra again emphasizes the power of the land, when she says to Carl, who has now returned again and is about to become her husband, "We come and go, but the land is always here." Carl tells her that she belongs to the land, "now more than ever." She implies that even if she might belong to the land, she could never fully own it: "I might as well try to will the sunset over there to my brother's children." And yet, her ownership of land, lots of it, is what gave her the resources to prosper. Although *O Pioneers!* has often been seen as a celebration of life on the frontier, including all the hard work that entails, success is bestowed on those who understand how to manipulate markets, how to buy and sell on the margin, and how to wait for commodities to increase in value—practices most associated with urban centers of finance.

Things to Think About

This chapter presents an alternative interpretation of pioneers and life on the frontier in Willa Cather's *O Pioneers!* Also, we have looked at only one aspect of this novel. As you read *O Pioneers!* or other works by Willa Cather, consider the following discussion questions:

1. What encounters have you had with the American West in fiction, film, essays, or video games? How have you responded to representations of pioneers?
2. How is the setting of this novel different from other texts you have read that have a more explicitly urban setting? Does *O Pioneers!* present urban spaces as dangerous?
3. In part two of the novel, Carl says "Isn't it queer: there are only two or three human stories, and they go on repeating themselves as fiercely as if they had never happened before; like the larks in this country, that have been singing the same five notes over for thousands of years." What do you make of this statement? What might those two or three stories be?

Things to Explore

Those who would like to learn more about Willa Cather and her works might consider the following texts:

1. *The Song of the Lark*. This novel, the second of Cather's prairie trilogy, tells the story of a young woman born in the West who eventually becomes a major opera singer. Like Alexandra Bergson, Thea Kronborg becomes enormously successful, and she is supported in her efforts along the way by several important male figures who encourage her to develop her artistry.
2. *My Ántonia*. Told from the perspective of a first-person narrator, Jim Burden, the third novel of the prairie trilogy is perhaps the most nostalgic for the American West. The primary focus

is on the struggles of immigrant homesteaders, particularly the hardships suffered by women.

3. Willa Cather National Center. The Willa Cather Foundation (www.WillaCather.org) maintains the center and website and provides many educational resources, along with programming in the restored Red Cloud Opera House and conservation of the Willa Cather Memorial Prairie.
4. The Willa Cather Archive at the University of Nebraska: cather.unl.edu/. The archive includes the journal *Cather Studies* and many other scholarly sources.

References

Cather, Willa. (1913) 2008. *O Pioneers!* Project Gutenberg. Last updated March 9, 2018. http://www.gutenberg.org/files/24/24-h/24-h.htm.

Cather, Willa. (1915) 2008. *The Song of the Lark*. Project Gutenberg. Last updated March 9, 2018. http://www.gutenberg.org/files/44/44-h/44-h.htm.

Cather, Willa. (1918) 2008. *My Ántonia*. Project Gutenberg. Last updated October 6, 2016. www.gutenberg.org/files/242/242-h/242-h.htm.

Fadiman, Clifton. 1932. "Willa Cather: The Past Recaptured," *The Nation* 6(December): 563–65.

Hinman, Eleanor. 1921. "Willa Cather, Famous Nebraska Novelist, Says Pioneer Mother Held Greatest Appreciation of Art—Raps Women Who Devote Themselves to Culture Clubs." *Lincoln Sunday Star*, 6 November.

"The Hundred Best Books of The Year." Review of *O Pioneers! The New York Times Book Review*, 30 November 1913, R664. https://timesmachine.nytimes.com/timesmachine/1913/11/30/issue.html.

Jefferson, Thomas. 1800. "From Thomas Jefferson to Benjamin Rush. 23 September 1800." *Founders Online*, National Archives. founders.archives.gov/documents/Jefferson/01-32-02-0102.

Limerick, Patricia. 1987. *The Legacy of Conquest*. New York: Norton.

Knopf, Alfred A. 1975. "Miss Cather." In *The Art of Willa Cather*, edited by Bernice Slote and Virginia Faulkner, 205–24. Lincoln: University of Nebraska Press.

O'Brien, Sharon. 1988. "Becoming Noncanonical: The Case against Willa Cather." *American Quarterly* 40(1): 110–26.

Sabao, Collen. 2014. "Towards a theory of genre? Reflections on the problems and debates on theorising 'genre.'" *The Dyke* 8(2): 1–19.

Slotkin, Richard. 1973. *Regeneration through Violence: The Mythology of the American Frontier, 1600–1860*. Middletown, CT: Wesleyan University Press.

Turner, Frederick Jackson. (1920) 2007. "The Significance of the Frontier in American History." In *The Frontier in American History*, 177–204. New York: Henry Holt. Project Gutenberg. http://www.gutenberg.org/files/22994/22994-h/22994-h.htm.

Willa Cather National Center. N.d. "About the Willa Cather Foundation." http://www.willacather.org/about-willa-cather-foundation.

Willa Cather National Center. N.d. "About Red Cloud." https://www.willacather.org/visit/red-cloud.

CHAPTER EIGHT

THE POETIC CITY: THE IMPORTANCE OF THE CITY SETTING IN *THE POET X*

Katie Sluiter

AT THE BEGINNING of each new school year, I share with my students Rudine Sim Bishop's (1990) theory that books can serve as mirrors, windows, and sliding doors. Our district is considered urban. However, compared to large cities such as Detroit, Chicago, or New York City, we are very tiny. Students often carry a misconception that because there are affluent, more rural districts just miles away, ours therefore is less than. Few of my students have ever traveled more than 100 miles away unless they have gone to visit family in Mexico or Latin America. These misconstructions are compiled by students being exposed to protagonists in literature, television, and film who are either white or a tired stereotype of a person of color and whose narratives and circumstances affirm these generalizations. Students are neither seeing themselves or accurate representations of those unlike themselves. Bishop agrees, contending that for too long, nonwhite children have not been able to find mirror texts, which means white students have an overabundance but do not have as much access to windows. Therefore, it is imperative to find texts that can serve as mirrors, windows, and hopefully sliding doors for students to participate viscerally in a broad array and representations of settings and experiences.

New York City is perhaps the most popular city in the world and one that often gets represented unfairly as dark and gritty and dangerous, or it is shown as a destination—a place that holds possibility and hope. Young adult author Elizabeth Acevedo, who was born and raised in a neighborhood near Harlem, paints a much different city, one that is inseparable from both the main character and plot of her debut novel, *The Poet X* (2018a). She creates a city that is comfortable and familiar and beautiful and part of who her protagonist, tenth-grader Xiomara Batista, is.

Living in Harlem with her Dominican parents and twin brother, Xiomara simultaneously feels unheard and exposed since her body grew curves. Although she tends to speak with her fists in response to what is said to and about her, everything else she writes about in her leather journal in the form of poetry: her mother's pious expectations, her father's disengagement, and the feelings she has for her lab partner in biology. Acevedo skillfully weaves both the freedom and claustrophobia of growing up in Harlem into her poetry about the paradoxes of coming of age. Many students will not only see themselves mirrored in Xiomara's experiences growing up, but they will peer through the window into an urban setting that lives and breathes alongside the characters.

In this chapter, I unpack the urban setting in *The Poet X* to show how place in a story is not just where things happen but rather a representation of the characters and movements of the story itself. I outline before-, during-, and after-reading activities that help students to consider the impact an urban setting such as New York City has on a writer's word choice, tone, and message, as well as provide writing opportunities for students to explore certain biases they may hold about urban settings or the people who live in them compared to how place fits in their own life stories.

Xiomara's story is hard to put down for sure, and the depiction of Harlem is both beautiful and poignant; however, there are other reasons that *The Poet X* (Acevedo 2018a) belongs in English Language Arts classrooms. Besides breaking the stereotype of a dark, gritty city lacking outdoor activities, Acevedo writes a moving story with universal and timely topics for students to see themselves in such as miscommunication and tension with parents and their expectations, sibling love and rivalry, and first love. Through her rich verse, she creates not only a window to gaze through for students who have not experienced the city in such a vibrant way but a sliding door for teenagers to ice skate alongside Xiomara and join her family and friends in the audience for open-mic night. The poetry not only tells a story but also brings readers into a place.

Preparing Students to Read

To center New York City, and more specifically Harlem, as a focus of the novel study, students can first explore their own preconceptions of what New York City and/or Harlem is like. One way to have students' answers made visual is to use a word-cloud maker site like wordclouds.com. If students are asked to type words they think of when they think about New York City or Harlem, the teacher can simply copy and paste all the responses into the site, and the site will generate a word cloud of all the words, making the most repeated words larger. The largest words in the cloud are the ones most students used in their responses. Posting these word clouds around the classroom can quickly show student thinking.

A natural activity to follow the word cloud is for students to investigate the representations of the city in media such as movies, television, music, and other literature. Classes can be divided into four groups, with each group in charge of exploring one of the four mediums. Each group will be given a large sheet of chart paper to collect words and images from their assigned medium. Once complete, the chart paper can be hung in the room alongside the student-generated word clouds. Students can then do a gallery walk taking notes on how each medium's representation of New York City compares and contrasts with the others and with the class's perception of the city. After the gallery walk, students can write a response followed by sharing out as a class. These artifacts can hang throughout the novel study as a way to bring students back to how New York is perceived by others in comparison to how Acevedo portrays it through Xiomara's poetry.

Even with books that serve as windows, students need to be able to find some sort of connection if they are going to be able to fully engage and hopefully, use the text as a sliding door. In her book *Reading, Writing, and Rising Up: Teaching about Social Justice and the Power of the Written Word,* Linda Christensen

(2000) provides different writing opportunities for students to explore how place contributes to their own stories. Before reading about New York City, students can explore stereotypes and false impressions outsiders might have of their own community. Young adult author Mark Oshiro (2019) has stated that "stereotypes are incomplete stories." Students can explore what the "incomplete stories" about their community might be through partner talk and writing prompts. Just as the artifacts showing the preconceived ideas about New York hang in the room during the novel study, so, too, should the student-generated stereotypes about their own community.

Supporting Learning while Reading

In part I of their book *Disrupting Thinking: Why How We Read Matters*, Kylene Beers and Robert E. Probst (2017) define "The Readers We Want" as being responsive, responsible, and compassionate. As students are guided through *The Poet X* (Acevedo 2018a), they can be encouraged to grow as readers in all of these areas through the lens of disrupting stereotypes of the urban setting that is Harlem, New York. Beers and Probst insist that students should be changed by what they read: "We want [students] to realize that reading should involve disrupting their thinking, changing their understandings of the world and themselves" (60). To do this, students need to be immersed in the text and encouraged to ask questions and dialogue with others. This section proposes various strategies and activities that can be used to help students plunge into both the text and their own thinking.

Although a 300-page book may seem daunting to most students, *The Poet X* (Acevedo 2018a) can be read relatively quickly due to the compact structure of a novel in verse and the quick-paced plot advancement Acevedo creates. Poems, however, are meant to be heard—especially those that are written for slam. Because the sound of her words is intertwined with the meaning of her words, listening to all or even selections of the audio version read by Acevedo (2018b) herself is recommended.

The first poem in the novel works as a way to situate the reader into Xiomara's place: a neighborhood in Harlem. Acevedo has spoken about the importance of place in her writing and how where the story takes place affects how the text is written saying, "[P]lace gives us [the readers and writers] the rhythm" and each place "has a different momentum" (Groenke 2019). In fact, Xiomara never sets down a poem that informs the reader all about Harlem or New York. She tells her own story and Harlem is a part of it. Again, Acevedo does this purposefully: "Characters know this home," she says, pointing out that her characters aren't going to explain the setting; rather, they will show it. "I expect students to do a little work, especially when it comes to place," she adds (Groenke 2019). For the purpose of doing "a little work," it would be helpful if students had a copy of the first poem, "Stoop-Sitting," printed on something they can annotate because this will be the poem that launches their exploration of the urban setting in *The Poet X*.

In his book *Write Like This*, Kelly Gallagher (2011) makes a case for teaching students to "move past first-draft thinking and into deeper levels of cognition" by teaching them to read through a piece more than once, looking for new levels in each pass (143). Using "Stoop-Sitting," students are separated into groups of three. During the first reading, one student reads aloud to the group as the other two mark words or phrases they find confusing. Students have a brief discussion about what they marked, possibly answering questions for each other or looking up word meanings (there are Spanish words included in many of the poems in the novel). Another student reads the poem through a second time. This time, the other two in the group are marking what they did not notice during the first reading. Again, a limited time to debrief follows. The procedure is repeated a last time with the third student in the group. Each group can then make a list of the imagery in the poem. The class then comes together to share out the imagery of Xiomara's Harlem. Students are then invited to look back at the artifacts that they found of stereotypes of the city and decide whether each instance of imagery confirms or refutes what they found before reading. This activity can be repeated throughout the reading of the novel whenever there is a specific poem that can be analyzed for the representation of Harlem/New York City.

A strategy that can be used throughout the reading of the novel is the "Book, Head, Heart" framework conceived by Beers and Probst (2017) in *Disrupting Thinking*. The three parts of this framework work especially well for texts such as poetry that lend themselves to responsive interpretation by the reader. Each area of the framework proposes questions to students to help them discern what the text is saying—both literally and implied—as well as whether their thinking or feelings have been challenged by what they read (63). These questions are especially helpful for students who may struggle beyond surface-level plot comprehension and work well as "quickwrite" writing prompts that can lead to partner talking and full-class discussions about what Xiomara is really saying in each of her poems, as well as what she is saying about her city home. The poem "After" (Acevedo 2018a, 52–53) is an example of a poem that works well as an activity for students to reflect on the layers of meaning in the text. There are multiple ideas students are required to think about while reading this poem: what "it" is, as well as what each of the places she lists is like and why "it" might happen there. Similarly, the poem "Mami Works" (Acevedo 2018a, 11) is a good poem for introducing the part of the framework that encourages students to think "beyond the text" (Beers and Probst 2017, 66). Students can discuss the parts of the poem that challenged their thinking about the city: the differences between Queens and Harlem, city transportation, and safety in the city. The poems "Open Mic Night" and "Signed Up" (Acevedo 2018a, 276–78) of the novel are good examples of poems to use for students to evaluate how they have grown and changed in response to reading *The Poet X* (Beers and Probst 2017, 68) This pair of poems is found in the last section of the novel, after students have had a good amount of exposure to Acevedo's city language. The scene is set in the real Nuyorican Poets Cafe on the lower east side of Manhattan. Students can apply all the parts of the framework to these pieces, even leading them to explore the cafe's website and why Elizabeth Acevedo would choose this venue for Xiomara's spoken word debut.

An additional activity that can be utilized to analyze how Acevedo uses place-based sensory language to characterize the city compared to the ways students found the city to be characterized in other media is student-created analyzing and interpretation charts (Gallagher 2011, 138). In groups of four, students can create a chart that is a 6 × 6 table. The top five headings are from the prereading activities exploring how the city has been represented or stereotyped by others: Ours, Television, Movies, Music, Other Literature, and Poet X. The headings for the six rows are Buildings, Outside Areas, Transportation, School, Housing, and Safety. Together, student groups fill in the chart with words or drawings that represent how each of the top headings represents each of the side headings. This activity can be done on chart paper to give room for creating the drawings and possibly including some of the words. After creating the charts and armed with notebooks and pencils, students can do a silent Gallery Walk of all the charts created in class. As they go from chart to chart, students can jot down the noticings and wonderings they have. After a set amount of time, the class comes back together to share what students notice and wonder about the depictions of the city in other media compared to how Acevedo portrays it through Xiomara's poetry.

Postreading Opportunities

Given that *The Poet X* (Acevedo 2018a) takes place in a city so widely written about in poetry as New York, there are many opportunities for students to further examine and explore ways poets have represented this city lyrically. One way to do this is to use a technique called a Jigsaw. The goal of a Jigsaw is that the assignment is organized so that students need to work together in order to be successful. For this NYC Poetry Jigsaw, students will be placed in groups of four. Each student in the group is given a different poem about New York: "Theme For English B" by Langston Hughes (1951), "Harlem Shadows" by Claude McKay (1922), "Autumn in New York" performed by Billie Holiday (1954), and "Skating in Harlem, Christmas Day" by Cynthia Zarin (2002) are possible choices. Students are given a set amount of time to do a first-draft read of their assigned, poem looking to make meaning and to find vocabulary they are not familiar with. They are then given some time to do a second-draft reading to find anything they may have missed during the first read-through, annotating the poem as they read.

For the third-draft reading, students meet with others in the class who have been assigned their same poem. They read and mark the text together, this time looking for connections to Elizabeth Acevedo's descriptions of the city and poetic techniques through Xiomara's poetry. Finally, students get back in their original group. Each group member takes a turn presenting their assigned poem to their group. The group then has a discussion about all the poems and how they compare to *The Poet X*. This can also turn into a larger-group discussion about point of view (two of the poets chosen and Black men from the Harlem Renaissance, one a female jazz singer from the 1920s and one a seventy-two-year-old white woman). Discussions about #OwnVoices and how it matters who is telling the story can be a rich addition to a study centered on the depiction of urban settings in literature and beyond (Yorio 2018).

The transition from reading poetry and writing poetry can be a smooth one if students are seeing the passages they read as mentor texts (Gallagher 2011, 20). Reading a novel in verse and subsequently reading poetry by other writers give students a bountiful set of poetic moves and techniques in their writer toolboxes. Whether students come from urban, suburban, or rural communities, they can all relate to using their voice to describe their place in the world as Xiomara did in *The Poet X* (Acevedo 2018a). Similarly, like Xiomara, sharing place-based writing can help create a closer community of learners. Linda Christensen (2000) says she works to "find space for [students'] lives to become part of the curriculum . . . by inviting them to write about their lives, about the worlds from which they come" (19).

Working from Kelly Gallagher's (2011) method of providing mentor texts for student writing, students will start by rereading the poem "H.S." from *The Poet X* (Acevedo 2018a, 35). Paying special attention to the form of the poem—non-rhyming couplets—and mimicking the stanza topics, students will write poems about their own school. Because all the students will be writing about the same topic, the end result will be one place from possibly twenty or more points of view. Depending on where the students are located, their "H.S." poems may be very similar to Xiomara's school, but they have the potential to be incredibly different. Both of these situations open the door for powerful conversations. In what ways is Xiomara's school a mirror to the students' school? In what ways is it a window? Do any of the students feel like they have walked through a sliding door? This writing can be made more personal by switching up the mentor poem. One possibility is "Ice-Skating" (Acevedo 2018a, 184). The structure of the poem can again be mimicked—four stanzas, the first two with four lines each, the third with six lines, and the fourth with five lines plus an indented line. Students can be asked to think of something they did as children that was special that they no longer do anymore. Using Acevedo's writing as their guide, students will create personal, narrative poems.

Poetry can be used not only for students to explore the settings of their own stories, but also to further examine those of fictional characters as well. Linda Christensen (2009) devotes a chapter in *Teaching for Joy and Justice* in using poetry to examine characters more deeply, stating, "Sometimes writing a poem or interior monologue from history or literature can create a space in the classroom for a different way of knowing, a different way of expressing knowledge about a fictional character or a historical decision" (50). One way to use this concept with *Poet X* (Acevedo 2018a) is to have students take the perspective of characters other than Xiomara and write poems about the city from those character points of view. For example, students could use the poem "Warmth" (116) and rewrite it from Aman's perspective of walking from the smoke park to the train station. Another way to do this activity is to use one of the mentor poems that Christensen (2009, 51) uses such as the metaphor poem. In Christensen's example, students take a human character from literature and create a metaphor for that character. To adapt this idea for use with *The Poet X*, students will look at how Xiomara uses urban images to detail her everyday life. For example, in the poem "The Next Couple Weeks" (Acevedo 2018a, 117), Xiomara opens her poem by writing, "Pass by like an express train" to describe how quickly the "next couple weeks" go by. This seemingly small simile shows how the city is part of who Xiomara is. Students can reread poems searching for such imagery and then create metaphor poems from those. For this particular example, students could create poems that begin with "time is an express train" and continue from there. This will not only give students a hands-on lesson in using rhetorical devices, but it will serve to expose how much where we are from seeps into our everyday speech. If Xiomara was in rural upstate New York rather than in Harlem, it is doubtful that she would compare time to an express train.

Another way students can use Christensen's (2009) idea of writing from a character's point of view is to write from the perspective of Harlem. To do this, students truly have to walk through Rudine Sims Bishop's sliding door. Christensen gives two good mentor poems for doing this: "Write That I . . ." and "Mirror Poems" (52). In both, the writer takes on the identity of Harlem. In the first, students begin the poem with the line "Write That I . . ." and the rest of the poem chronicles how the speaker—in this case, the city—wants to be remembered. The second type takes it a step further: students consider Lucille Clifton's poem "what the mirror said" (1980) to write a poem about what a mirror would reflect, in this case if they were the city of Harlem looking into the mirror (Christensen 2009, 52). Students can be required to use bits of Xiomara's story in these poems or not, depending on the extent to which they want these poems to reflect their understanding of the novel or of the urban setting itself.

Poetry slams are described in the novel, but the most detailed and structurally interesting in "At the New York Citywide Slam" (Acevedo 2018a, 353), where Xiomara illustrates the moment when she gets on stage for the big citywide slam. What better way to bring the unit together in a culminating response to the novel than students writing and performing their own slam poetry? Lindsay Ann of Lindsay Ann Learning (2019) gives twelve tips for teaching slam poetry in the English classroom on her blog including listening and discussing slam poetry. Listening to Elizabeth Acevedo (2018b) read parts of *The Poet X* will give students a feel for Xiomara's voice, but they will want to hear others as well. Classroom-friendly poets who can be found on YouTube include Phil Kaye, Sarah Kay, Harry Baker, Lamar Jordan, and Clint Smith. Students should study the topics and length of slam poems, as well as research the New York slam-poetry scene to see what performing specifically in New York would be like. The final poetry slam could be an in-class recitation by volunteers or a larger event in which parents and community members are invited.

Things to Think About

Regardless of whether the students reading *The Poet X* are in urban, rural, or suburban settings, by reading Xiomara's poems and writing some of their own, they will be able to walk through sliding doors and experience something new to them. Besides looking strictly at the city setting, there are other lenses teachers can place in front of students as they view the scenery Acevedo paints through well-placed questioning:

1. How does Xiomara's Dominican culture affect what is included in her poems?
2. Because Xiomara's mother is a devout Catholic, Xiomara spends a lot of time in church. How do the Catholic churches in Harlem and their atmosphere in the neighborhood affect the tone of Xiomara's poems?
3. East Harlem has been gentrified in recent years. Where are hints of this in the novel and how does it affect Xiomara's family?

Things to Explore

Other resources for teaching *The Poet X*, slam poetry, and other urban Latina works include the following:

1. Harper Teen has an Educator's Guide for teaching *The Poet X*.
2. Scholastic's website has lesson plans for teaching slam poetry to middle grade students.
3. Sandra Cisneros, *The House on Mango Street* (New York: Knopf Doubleday Publishing Group, 1984) with Jago, Carol, *Sandra Cisneros in the Classroom* (Urbana: National Council of Teachers of English, 2002) for urban Chicano vignettes
4. Erica L. Sánchez, *I Am Not Your Perfect Mexican Daughter* (New York: Alfred A. Knopf, 2017), for urban Latina prose.

References

Acevedo, Elizabeth. 2018a. *The Poet X*. New York: Harper Collins USA.

Acevedo, Elizabeth. 2018b. *The Poet X*. Audiobook. Narrated by Elizabeth Acevedo. New York: Quill Tree Books.

Beers, G. Kylene, and Robert E. Probst. 2017. *Disrupting Thinking: Why How We Read Matters*. New York: Scholastic.

Bishop, Rudine Sims. 1990. "Mirrors, Windows, and Sliding Glass Doors." *Perspectives* 6(3): ix–xi.

Christensen, Linda. 2000. *Reading Writing, and Rising Up: Teaching about Social Justice and The Power of the Written Word*. Milwaukee, WI: Rethinking Schools.

Christensen, Linda. 2009. *Teaching for Joy and Justice: Re-Imagining the Language Arts Classroom*. Milwaukee, WI: Rethinking Schools Publication.

Clifton, Lucille. 1980. "what the mirror said." In *Two-Headed Woman*. University of Massachusetts Press.

Duke, Vernon. *Autumn in Harlem*. 1954. Billie Holiday. Clef MGC 161 / Verve MGC 686 / LDB.23.

Gallagher, Kelly. 2011. *Write like This: Teaching Real-World Writing through Modeling & Mentor Texts*. Portsmouth, NH: Stenhouse.

Groenke, Susan. 2019. "Interview with Elizabeth Acevedo." ALAN Conference, Baltimore, MD. November 25.

Hughes, Langston. 1951. "Theme for English B." In *Montage of a Dream Deferred*. New York: Henry Holt and Company.

Lindsay Ann Learning. 2019. "12 Slam Poetry Ideas for Teachers: English Teacher Blog." *Lindsay Ann Learning English Teacher Blog*, October 28. http://lindsayannlearning.com/teaching slam-poetry/.

McKay, Claude. 1922. "Harlem Shadows." In *Harlem Shadows*. New York: Harcourt, Brace and Company.

Oshiro, Mark. 2019. "The Danger of a Single Story." Panel discussion at the National Council of Teachers of English Conference, November 21–24, Baltimore, MD.

Yorio, Kara. 2018. "#OwnVoices Not Familiar to All." *School Library Journal*, October 23. http://www.slj.com/?detailStory=ownvoices-not-familiar-all.

Zarin, Cynthia. 2002. "Skating in Harlem, Christmas Day." In *The Watercourse*. New York: Knopf.

CHAPTER NINE

An Author's Perspective: An Undocumented Girl Finds a Sense of Belonging

Maria Andreu

I DON'T REMEMBER my first memory of New York City. Growing up in its outskirts, in an illegal basement apartment across the Hudson in New Jersey, the city was always in the warp and weft of my experience. My parents, young twenty-somethings who overstayed their visitors' visas to carve out a life in the city's shadow economy, always held it in fascination. There are pictures of me in a putty-green stroller in front of an unfinished World Trade Center and of me sitting on a cannon overlooking the Hudson toward the city, the skyline a mythical backdrop to pictures of my first lost tooth. Later, when my mother and I traveled to my parents' native Argentina for a funeral and couldn't get back to the United States for two years, it was New York City I thought of when I imagined the things I wanted to "go home" to do. For someone who had a childhood full of feeling like I didn't belong anywhere, New York sure did feel a lot like home.

Growing up undocumented in the United States, there was much I knew didn't belong to me. My mother hushed me when I spoke Spanish in the supermarket, lest I draw attention to us. I'd had to skip kindergarten, before our departure for Argentina when I was six, because American school wasn't for me. My parents were afraid of the residency requirements for enrollment, so they kept me home, even though I'd been reading since age four and spinning tales that read suspiciously like the Disney book of fairy tales whose edges I'd made dark with smudgy fingerprints. Our basement home was rented. The car my father drove us around in was the cab he used to make money, and it didn't belong to us either.

But New York . . . New York belonged to me.

New York belonged to me when my parents, who didn't always have money for the electricity bill, took me into Macy's of Fifth Avenue for my winter coats. New York belonged to me even in the distance, when we walked down to the river to watch the fireworks or to marvel at the regatta for the bicentennial. My childhood was infused with the scent of exclusion and going to New York felt like being able to sneak into the world of the fairies and the magicians. It carved me and knew me. And I knew it.

One of my earliest acts of rebellion was sneaking into New York City with some friends when I told my mother I'd be somewhere else, probably at the library. It was good to grow up free-range, with access to the fifty-cent bus and the PATH train and unrestricted by the shackles of a cell phone. Barely fourteen, with no idea what to do, we clung close to the station where we'd emerged from the train—West Eighth and Sixth Avenue—and wandered, wide-eyed, feeling brave, in and out of stores on just that block. We bought Marilyn Monroe postcards at the poster store and ate New York pizza. We stared googly-eyed at the spectacular shiny boots in a shoe store whose entrance was below ground level. On later forays, we rummaged through old coats at the Antique Boutique and Andy's Chee-pees a little further afield.

There was a lot of turmoil in my adolescence. Being undocumented brings with it a host of problems, like not knowing how I could ever manage to go to college, even though I was bookish and good grades came easily to me. Things at home were not great. I was itchy, restless, wanted more. My father demanded control. "If you could just be quiet," my mother counseled, "maybe he wouldn't hit so much." A rage, volcanic and mean, simmered in me, and I wanted to go, go, go.

Mostly where I wanted to go was New York City.

The city wore many costumes in my life: alluring, upscale place of shops I couldn't afford and grungy downtown art scene. When I was about sixteen, it seduced me with its night clubs, which, in the 1980s, were lax about our ridiculous fake IDs and let us into a thrumming, vibrant world where some guys were handsy but we were goddesses whose smiles garnered free drinks. During the height of my James Dean phase, the Museum of Broadcasting put on screenings of his obscure early work, bad made-for-television dramas they played in small rooms, seemingly just for me, because there was rarely anyone else in there. During my senior year of high school, when one of my best friends had reconstructive surgery at Sloan Kettering following a bout of childhood cancer, the city revealed to me its East Side and the ease with which you could sneak a patient out of the hospital for muffins. When my first boyfriend suggested we go into the Village for a date, the city introduced me to the Pride Parade, men in assless chaps, and the Ghost of Shakespeare who recited my favorite sonnet to us as we sat in Washington Square Park.

At the age of twelve I wrote in my diary, "Most of all, I want to be a writer." It would be a long slog for the girl without papers, the girl who didn't know how anything worked. When I was eighteen, the author of my life pulled a major *deus ex machina* that wouldn't work in any actual manuscript: an amnesty was passed and, poof, just like that, I wasn't undocumented anymore. But the vapor of its alienation and confusion clung to me for many years, most potently in my twenties as I tried to figure out my path. I left the rough home life behind that same year, finding a $200 a week job in Washington Heights. New York became sustenance then, not boys in nightclubs, but a paycheck.

It would be many years before I'd find my way to a writing career. Ironically, it came when I finally wrote about my biggest secret: my undocumented past. My debut young adult novel, *The Secret Side of Empty* (2014), tells the story of a girl living very much in the shadows, as I did. Although I set it in my native New Jersey, New York hovers like a dream, as it does in so much of what I write. In my forthcoming book, *Love in English*, my protagonist, a new immigrant flummoxed by the many strictures of her new language, has her happiest moment when she sneaks into New York City to take part in a poetry slam, to find her voice—much like New York helped me find mine.

I have traveled far from my days of the electricity getting cut off in the basement and of looking toward my future and seeing nothing but an inky void. I've seen, and been charmed by, many cities in the United States and in the world. Cities hold such allure because they are places of push and pull, of expression, of innovation and invention, where people thrown together learn to specialize and thrive.

It's not all ideal, of course. Cities are also where gentrification pushes lower-income people out, where wealth disparities can sometimes be on grotesque display. And yet I often lament to my children that the Forty-second Street they've known, with its glitzy, corporate logos and clean sidewalks, is a far cry from the rough, dirty one I knew in my teens. They never got to experience the muttered offers of "nickel-dime" from dealers who didn't make eye contact and the eye-popping storefronts promising Girls Girls Girls and other debaucheries that titillated and scared us. As a mother, I'm glad they're in the safe New York. But, as a teenager, the place of grit and grime was an education, a thrill, a challenge. I wouldn't have given up that experience for anything—not the marriage proposal from the homeless guy at the Port Authority as we waited for the bus home from a club at 3 a.m., not the spray-painted subways where I once saw a guy stagger off bleeding, not the Drug Enforcement Administration raids regularly conducted on the block across the street from my first job. As far as preparation for being a novelist, it did not get much better than New York in the 1980s.

New York has given me a lifetime of stories. It finds its way into my fantasy worlds in the bustle of the main trading town. I draw from my many nights there when I want to write a scene about freedom, about what it feels like to first be loosed from parental control. I imagine its lights, and its streets, even when I am writing about elsewhere. For a girl who once belonged nowhere, New York has helped me, through its trial by fire, to feel comfortable anywhere. It's not the only education for being a writer, but it was mine, and I'm grateful for it.

References

Andreu, Maria E. 2014. *This Side of Empty*. Philadelphia: Running Press Teens.
Andreu, Marie E. Forthcoming. *Love in English*. New York: Balzer + Bray.

CHAPTER TEN

The Urban and the Urbane: Girls and New York City in Cecily von Ziegesar's *Gossip Girl* and Rita Williams-Garcia's *Jumped*

Emma K. McNamara

SIDE BY SIDE, Cecily von Ziegesar's (2002) *Gossip Girl* and Rita Williams-Garcia's (2009) *Jumped* look quite similar: both books are set in urban areas, rely on bullying as a personality trait, have girls enrolled in accelerated high school courses, focus on physical appearance and fashion, and are built on unreliable narrators. However, *Gossip Girl* is deemed glamorous—just listen to the television show's theme song—whereas *Jumped* is deemed unalluring. The covers of the books even refer to the inside contents as "elite" versus "gritty," respectively. As historian Mario Maffi (2004) says, "the history of New York and its image is a 'never-ending story'—maybe because the city is so full of stories that it is impossible to capture them all through the written word alone" (97)—*Gossip Girl* and *Jumped* might at first look quite similar, yet their contents could not be presented more differently.

Jumped (Williams-Garcia 2009), a fast-paced National Book Award finalist, takes place during one school day wherein Leticia overhears Dominique say she is going to beat up Trina after school because Dominique feels that Trina was being disrespectful by walking between Dominique and two friends in the hallway before school started. Leticia has all day to tell an adult who will hopefully prevent the beating from happening, but Leticia likes knowing this juicy gossip before everyone else and decides that Dominique's problem with Trina is not her business in which to meddle. Trina has no idea that Dominique is angry or that she will be beaten into a coma by the end of the day.

Gossip Girl, a series "developed by a production company [that] sought the highest literary bidder," follows, via the panoptical namesake narrator, a slew of wealthy Upper East Side, Manhattan teenagers (Pattee 2006, 155). In the first book in the series, *Gossip Girl* (von Ziegesar 2002), It-Girl Serena van der Woodsen returns to Manhattan and the Constance Billard School for Girls after a year away at boarding school, freshman Jenny Humphrey attempts to be part of the popular crowd, and Blair Waldorf, Serena's best friend, mulls losing her virginity to her boyfriend Nate Archibald.

"Well it all started off on 8th Avenue"/ "When I made up the name called the Get Fresh Crew"

The teenage experience in *Gossip Girl* (von Ziegesar 2002) and *Jumped* (Williams-Garcia 2009) is at once completely identical and wildly different. The characters worry about how they look, who likes them, who is attracted to them, how they will market themselves for the best chance at a future, and how to not take the negative aspects of their lives too seriously. Because "one must acknowledge the limitation of any single storyline that proposes to interpret the 'urban'" (Judd and Simpson 2011, 16), it is important to remember that New York City is composed of so many things: Times Square, Bloomingdales, the Apollo Theater, Coney Island. To insinuate that multiple stories, that multiple lives are not happening concurrently, would be irresponsible. The city that is the first image of the American dream that proudly displays the foremost symbol of both struggle and success is equally home to Blair, Serena, Dominique, Leticia, and Trina, an intricate intersection of the teenage girl.

Before child labor laws went into effect, one was either a child or an adult; the concept of the teenager is a relatively new phenomenon. Requiring adolescents to attend school creates a teenaged space. To be sure, "without high school, there are no teenagers" (Hine 1999, 139). The concept and space of high school are critical for them to distance themselves from their parents while still being in a safe, controlled environment. Teenagers need high school to practice different identities: a basketball player, an artist, a film director, a writer.

"We have become so accustomed to the idea that high school should be the universal experience of our youth that we don't even consider other possibilities" (Hine 99, 139). How, then, can the lives depicted in *Gossip Girl* (von Ziegesar 2002) and the lives depicted in *Jumped* (Williams-Garcia 2009) take place a mere few blocks apart? Each of these books relies heavily on the characters' high school experiences, which are considerably similar, yet those experiences could not be more different. Both *Gossip Girl* and *Jumped*'s similarities and differences can be true because "the city of New York rejects the static and the fixed, and in order to integrate oneself successfully within the city, one must be open to all kinds of change and renewal" (Carroll 2014, 98).

Both Serena and Trina are able to move fluidly in their spaces and have different interests and friends, while Blair and Dominique have set ways regarding how things are done and get upset when someone in their path is able to deviate since it is not so easy for them to do so. Blair is angry at Serena because she believes Serena floats through life effortlessly. Dominique rules her life with a simple code: "I'm not in your face, don't be in mine. My rules are simple. Don't mess with me, I don't mess with you" (Williams-Garcia 2009, 33). Dominique asserts her opinion in no uncertain terms.

"Teenagers occupy a special place in the society. They are envied and sold to, studied and deplored. They are expected to break some rules, but there are other restrictions that apply only to them. They are at a golden moment in life—and not to be trusted" (Hine 1999, 10). Leticia lies to the assistant principal about knowing what happened in the fight and knows how to ask a question in class to make it look like she has done her homework; Dominique has sex in public and tries to get her teachers to cheat for her; Trina flirts with classmates to get them to do her work for her; Blair does not update Serena's address to purposely leave her out of receiving a fundraiser invitation; Serena has sex with her best friend's boyfriend; Jenny Humphrey only offers to make Blair's fundraiser invitations so she can ensure she will be invited; the girls wear their uniform kilts shorter than the dress code permits; Nate ignores Blair's emails and phone calls to get high and not deal with how high-strung she is. Although these teenagers are inherently good people, they all have a sneaky side; they will not be held accountable for their mischief, because "one of the mystique's key assumptions [is] what teenagers do doesn't really count" (Hine 1999, 15). They all know how to use people to get what they want, knowing that, because they are young and/or because they are wealthy.

"Teenagers are often expected to be transgressors, and when they do fail to conform to the frequently ambiguous rules within which they are expected to live, they can be punished very severely," says Hine (1999, 17). Dominique truly feels as though her life is over because she will not be able to play basketball again until the next school year. This severe punishment, missing playing minutes, decreasing stats, leaves her in despair. She is desperate. Her suspension is "life and death. Important" (Williams-Garcia 2009, 15). She begs her coach and multiple teachers throughout the day to raise her grades just a few points so she can cross the eligibility threshold and play again. She is not asking for a huge raise: "all I need is to be up a few points and I get my time back," she pleads to a teacher (Williams-Garcia 2009, 17). Oozing helplessness, she tells the reader, "Here I am, pleading my heart out like a stupid bitch" (Williams-Garcia 2009, 17).

Hine (1999) offers that "[t]eenagers spend much of their lives dealing with people who do not know them as individuals, and under the control of institutions that strive to deal with people uniformly" (17). Dominique's coach's rules do not allow her to play basketball, and thus, she spirals downward, hard. But what if playing basketball is the only reason Dominique stays engaged at school? It is clear that basketball is the only thing she cares about, and although the concept of punishment is to take away something truly cared about for a lesson to be learned, it is also important that adults know what teenagers' lifelines are. The Social Interaction teacher writes in Dominique's file that "Dominique has skills on the court. A team sport will help her interact socially and learn to cooperate with others" (Williams-Garcia 2009, 35). Dominique needs to be an active player on the basketball team because "the loss of a stable sense of personal identity can be traumatic and unwelcome" (Carroll 2014, 98). Dominique spends all day on edge trying to figure out how to remedy her eligibility.

"These expensive, these is red bottoms"/ "These is bloody shoes"

New York City is "a space wherein old identifications can be put aside and new identities that respond to the crowd can be tested and explored" (Carroll 2014, 97). In *Jumped* (Williams-Garcia 2009), Trina wears a pink tracksuit and, throughout her day, shows it off to the assistant principal, the step team, and her drawing partner in art class. Her aesthetic, at least at the current moment, includes the color pink, and she shows off her clothes by doing a little shimmy. More than once, Trina comments that she knows, she just knows, she has brightened others' day just by looking good in her pink outfit. The juxtaposition of the casual clothing of *Jumped* versus the uniforms adorned with expensive accessories of *Gossip Girl* "makes the reader aware of social divisions within the city" (Carroll 2014, 108). In *Gossip Girl* (von Ziegesar 2002), Jenny Humphrey decides that to fit in at Constance Billard, she needs new clothes, even though she wears a uniform to school. Like many ninth graders, she wants to seem mature and grown up and not be mixed up with girls in younger grades. Throughout *Gossip Girl*, Jenny Humphrey is seen dragging her brother along to buy new clothes.

Because of the predication of *Gossip Girl*, the "details of the lives of the characters—and the characterization itself—are described in terms of commercial consumption" (Pattee 2006, 155). Everything the *Gossip Girl* (von Ziegesar 2002) characters wear and do have brand names and are described as such. Serena uses Urban Decay lip gloss and wears Pucci dresses. Kate Spade gift bags are presented to attendees of a fundraiser Blair is planning. The girls smoke Gauloise cigarettes and shop at Barneys. "Clothing becomes the medium through which the 'enfolding of identity and place' is expressed" (Carroll 2014, 99), and as such, the characters in *Gossip Girl* are always described based on what they are wearing, thereby positioning them as wealthy residents and Manhattan Elite.

To paint Serena as Other, and begin to both leave her out and make her feel left out, on her first day back at Constance Billard, her outfit is described as ratty: "She hadn't had a haircut in over a year. . . . Her boy's white oxford shirt was frayed on the collar and cuffs, and through it, her purple lace bra was visible. On her feet was her favorite pair of brown lace-up boots, and her black stockings had a big hole behind one knee" (von Ziegesar 2002, 44). Gossip Girl, the narrator, then tells the reader that Serena is wearing the new maroon polyester uniform kilt as opposed to the old navy wool one, thus cementing her as out of the loop even more. This is the only time her appearance is not linked to a list of high-end designer brand names.

These Streets Will Make You Feel Brand New

In a recent tweet, Houston mayor Sylvester Turner (2020) wrote that "cities are ultimately made up of two things—people and places." Similarly, Irish lecturer Jane Suzanne Carroll (2014) says, "landscape and identity are inextricably connected" (97). The city can hide its residents' secrets, can be a safe space for residents to practice different identities, can be a springboard for rebounding, and can guide those who desire to uncover its marvelous secrets. The city is haunting, terrifying, beautiful, and romantic. The city wants its residents to explore all reaches of its boundaries and energize them to explore all reaches of their own boundaries and even push them past their limits.

Cities are "constantly evolving organisms subject to the processes of growth and decay, interdependence, competition and cooperation, health, and disease" (Judd and Simpson 2011, 3). Friends since they were young girls, Blair and Serena's friendship is at once loyal and volatile. They, perhaps knowingly, perhaps unknowingly, compete for Nate's affection, for being the most looked-to girls in school, and for spots at Ivy League colleges. For almost two decades, they have grown together, they have missed one another when apart, and they have relied on the other for basic necessities. They have also hated and sabotaged each other, almost wasting moments together, a friendship decaying. Their friendship symbolizes what they love about their city, what their city's defining characteristics are. Blair and Serena are New York City; they embody all the reasons why people love and hate it.

Carroll (2014) says, "The individual does not have to be subsumed by the crowd but . . . if a person can learn to become a crowd by themselves—that is to acquire or develop multiplicitous personae that reflect the multiplicity of the city—they can retain some control over their identity" (99). In *Gossip Girl* (von Ziegesar 2002), Serena returns home from school one afternoon bored and lonely, feeling sorry for herself and moping around her massive penthouse apartment. While sifting through the mail, she finds a postcard for an art exhibit opening happening that very afternoon: "It was definitely cool, though. There was no question about it; Serena knew what she was doing for the next two hours" (88). Suddenly, Serena changes from her school uniform into black leather pants, immediately morphing into a Cool Girl, and "within minutes she was stepping out of a taxi in front of the Whitehot Gallery downtown in Chelsea" (89). At this exhibit, the artists take an immediate liking to Serena and photograph her for their next piece, "a new avant-garde public art program" to be displayed "on the sides of buses, in subways, and in the advertising boxes on top of taxis all over town" (91). In a matter of hours, Serena goes from hopeless to icon, showing that if you allow the multiplicity of the city to envelop you, you will be rewarded. Here, "the individual is open to the cycles of symbolic death and rebirth, negation and renewal" (Carroll 2014, 99). "Through all of [Serena's] troubles, the city of New York itself remains a constant friend and ally in her efforts to" reintegrate into Constance Billard and Manhattan (Fritz 2014, 88).

Gossip Girl and Leticia, both unreliable narrators, serve as the panoptical vision of action in each book. Whereas Gossip Girl posts her visions on her eponymous website, Leticia shares hers with her unseen friend Bea, who, in a way, acts as Leticia's conscience. Throughout the day, Bea continuously tells Leticia to either tell an adult about what she overheard or warn Trina or both. It is not entirely clear whether Bea is real or not. Additionally, Leticia does not seem to have other friends at school with whom she interacts within the space of *Jumped* (Williams-Garcia 2009). While *Jumped*'s chapters alternate between the perspectives of Leticia, Dominique, and Trina, only Leticia notices both girls. Dominique, of course, notices Trina but does not notice Leticia, and Trina notices neither. After Trina's beating, as the crowd of onlooking students disburses, the assistant principal says to Leticia, "[Y]ou seem to know what goes on. What can you tell me?"—insinuating further that Leticia is the omniscient eye in the school (161). Gossip Girl is constantly reporting what happens to Blair, Serena, Jenny, and Nate on her website, including when they are contained in one another's residences, not just when they are in public. Through Gossip Girl and Leticia, "the act of seeing in New York (the act of seeing New York)—on the streets, beneath the towers, inside the houses, in the tunnels, on the bridges, inside the kaleidoscope—once again become[s] a deeply emotional experience" (Maffi 2004, 90), as the reader worries what will happen to Trina, feels empathy for Serena, and watches the effects of the city affect the girl inhabitants.

At one point in *Gossip Girl* (von Ziegesar 2002), Nate and his friends skip gym class and lunch to go to Central Park during what might be one of the last beautiful days of fall: "It was a sunny October day in Central Park. Out in Sheep Meadow lots of kids were cutting school, just lying in the grass, smoking, or playing Frisbee. The trees surrounding the meadow were a blaze of yellows, oranges, and reds, and beyond the trees loomed the beautiful old apartment buildings on Central Park West" (77). Nate's friends pepper him with questions, asking whether he loves Blair or Serena more; von Ziegesar labels his responses with "longingly," "frowning," and "regretted" (78, 79). Finally, Nate gets high enough that he lays back in the grass, tunes his friends out, imagines Blair and Serena, and "smiled and closed his eyes" (80). The reader sees here that "the metropolis speaks to us with eloquence, and often violently so, but there is a dreamy or nightmarish quality to all this" (Maffi 2004, 96).

There is such a "physical bond with the street and city locations which, as we have seen, proved so important in New York literature" (Maffi 2004, 98). Every morning before school, the teenagers of Gossip Girl can be seen smoking cigarettes and drinking coffee on the steps of the Metropolitan Museum of Art. Even Dominique and her friends visit the food cart across the street from their school for bagels and hot chocolates before going to class. This ritual, which clearly spans racial and socioeconomic boundaries, is seen as a nonnegotiable part of their day, almost as if, were they to skip this daily transaction, they would feel as though they had neglected to do an important chore.

"And since kindygarten, I acquired the knowledge"/ "And after 12th grade, I went straight to college"

von Ziegesar based her *Gossip Girl* series on her alma mater, the Nightingale-Bamford School, which currently costs almost $53,000 each year in tuition (although the website claims 20 percent of the student body receives financial aid), has a 6:1 student-to-teacher ratio, and an average class size of twelve students. Of the six schools in which Williams-Garcia observed in her preparation to write *Jumped*—Beach Channel High School, Benjamin N. Cardozo High School, Brooklyn Community Arts and Media High School, DeWitt Clinton High School, Franklin K. Lane High School, and Thurgood Marshall High School—two have closed due to alleged poor performance. The ones that remain open have an average 26:1 student-to-teacher ratio, and over half of the student bodies receive free or reduced-price lunch. Gossip Girl's production company, 17th Street Productions, alludes to 17th Street in Brooklyn, which is situated in ritzy Park Slope, one of New York City's most desirable neighborhoods, whereas one can assume that, while *Jumped* was Williams-Garcia's third consecutive book to be published by HarperCollins, she did not receive a large amount of monetary support for its creation.

When modernizing Japan in the late nineteenth century, the Meiji government looked to Tokyo for its centrality and rising prominence, which led to the city becoming a cultural center that included a concentrated power for higher education (Young 2013, 37). In more rural areas, children stopped going to school at a young age to help with familial obligations; such behaviors were seen in America as well. Yet, in urban areas, and especially with the advent of child labor laws that began in America in 1904 and were federally upheld in 1938, children had to attend school until at least age sixteen. Urban historian Louise Young (2013) says, "in anointing certain cities as centers of modern knowledge, state educational policy created a cultural geography that concentrated human and material resources for knowledge production, in the process helping to constitute a system of centers and peripheries" (41). The school von Ziegesar based *Gossip Girl* on is situated on the Upper East Side of Manhattan, central in the whole of New York City. The schools Williams-Garcia based *Jumped* on are on the northern and eastern edges—the Bronx, Brooklyn, and Queens. To further differentiate schools, "status distinctions persisted between the first generation of 'number' schools and the expanded cadre of 'name schools'" (Young 2013, 43). In New York City, private schools have names, whereas public schools have numbers. Students must apply to enroll in all private schools, whereas some public schools require applications for magnet programs, and some do not. It is unclear which tier of public school the school in *Jumped* falls into, nor does Williams-Garcia give it a name, but the school offers both remedial and advanced courses.

The first public high school in New York City, Flushing High School, opened in 1875, almost 150 years after the first New York City private school, the Collegiate School, opened in 1628. Around 1930, employers began requiring that job seekers have high school diplomas, because "the nexus of knowledge and power [were] concentrated in secondary education" and "was one reason why localities were willing to commit scarce budgetary resources to establish a network of postelementary schools" (Young 2013, 42). Letitia talks about the thousands of feet that walk through the halls of her school each day, while the girls at Constance Billard attend numerous one-on-one meetings with the college advisers.

"Cross my path, I'll crush ya, thinking I won't touch ya"

Violence—feeling slighted, feeling disrespected, and wanting to hurt others either physically or emotionally—is a main theme of each book. While the violence in *Jumped* is manifested physically, the violence in *Gossip Girl* is manifested through bullying. Blair is hurt that Serena left for boarding school in the midst of Blair's parent's divorce, but does not want to tell Serena that for fear of sounding weak. Instead of talking to Serena, however, Blair decides to be mean and exclude Serena from all her social plans, decidedly making Serena feel left out. Although Serena is not being beaten into a coma like Trina, the violence against her is markedly traumatic. Emotional and mental violence is still metabolized strongly by the victim, and the perpetrator, here Blair, is just as devious and calculating as those who physically hurt others, such as Dominique. In 1997, "Zachary Brown, of the New York City Department of Health, found that young people saw violence as the most rational response available" (Thabit and Piven 2003, 99). Both Blair and Dominique have resources aplenty available to help them quell their rage, yet that is a less rational inclination to them than turning to violence.

Dominique, *Jumped*'s (Williams-Garcia 2009) antagonist, has been suspended from the school's basketball team for poor grades, academic ineligibility. Her story begins as she and two friends wait for a teacher to arrive at school to plead her case for him to raise her grade five points so she can play again. He refuses, telling Dominique that she is in charge of her marks, not him, and she becomes angry. This anger, which Dominique has not shaken, is what roils her when Trina walks between her and her friends, and thus sets the stage for Trina's beating. At the end of the novel, Dominique is interviewed from a correctional facility—it is unclear whether she is being held as a juvenile or as an adult—and she tells the interviewer that she is not sorry for beating Trina.

Dominique's story emphasizes research that tells us that "illiteracy ate away at [students] and was one of the prime causes for children's breaks with school, family, and, ultimately, society. Many such children became juvenile delinquents" (Thabit and Piven 2003, 88). This is somewhat complicated in Williams-Garcia's (2009) plot development because although Dominique is enrolled in a course called Social Interaction, in which she learns anger management skills, showing that the school believes she is predisposed to violent outbursts, in this instance, due to Dominique's unsatisfactory grades, she becomes a delinquent and is, quite literally, removed from "school, family, and, ultimately, society."

Ultimately, Dominique acts on her fury not because of being benched by her basketball coach but because she "can't let [Trina] cut into [her] like that. Through [her] space. Through [her]. Can't let that slide. She has to know, she can't do that. . . . It's all right, I'll handle it. Handle it. Set her straight. She'll learn" (Williams-Garcia 2009, 32). Dominique believes that "a quick and violent reaction may dissuade future attacks by onlookers" (Thabit and Piven 2003, 99) and that by "handling" Trina, her friends and others will not see her as easily taken advantage of. In the survey, students reported that "a beating subdues most impulses and is faster and easier than an explanation" (Thabit and Piven 2003, 99), since transgressors should already know what their transgression was. When Dominique beats up Trina at the end of the school day, between punches, she says, "[Y]ou see my face now, bitch?" (Williams-Garcia 2009, 159), instead of telling Trina that she thought walking between her and her friends was rude. Students "mostly drifted into doing bad things through peer pressure" (Thabit and Piven 2003, 99). Dominique feels compelled to beat Trina so nobody else in school thinks they can mess with her. She is unable to let Trina's unknowing indiscretion slide. She says, "[I]t's not that I *want* to respond to it, I *have* to respond to it" (Williams-Garcia 2009, 37).

"But—look around, look around"/ "the revolution's happening in New York"

In *Gossip Girl* and *Jumped*, von Ziegesar (2002) and Williams-Garcia (2009), respectively, elaborate on the notion that "there is no single clear path through the urban space, rather, the innumerable routes through the streets and paths intersect and diverge" (Carroll 2014, 98). Both of these narratives conform to

> the New York School that flourished in the latter decades of the twentieth century [and] was characterized by several distinguishing features: first, a strong interest in the central city, especially Manhattan; second, a determination to improve city life; third, a utopian belief that the central city could and should be a place where the wealthy, the middle class, the working class, and the poor can coexist; and fourth, a belief that city life is superior to suburban life. (Halle and Beveridge 2011, 139)

Blair, Serena, Dominique, Leticia, and Trina are "brash, unfinished, ebullient, idealistic, crude, energetic, innocent, greedy, changing in all sorts of unsettling ways" (Hine 1999, 10), and what a privilege it is that von Ziegesar and Williams-Garcia reveal each of their personalities for adolescent readers to befriend, to see themselves within, and to journey along with.

"Not for these reasons alone, but because right from the start it was precisely the landscape of New York . . . the street as a stage, the urban labyrinth, the continual movement, the incessant transformations, the sheer variety of its inhabitants, the overwhelming multitude of stories and events" (Maffi 2004, 98) that draws the reader into *Gossip Girl* and *Jumped*. The novels' pacing speeds by as quickly as a New York City taxi. Blair, Serena, Jenny Humphrey, Leticia, Dominique, and Trina could have crossed paths with one another without ever noticing. In fact, within their novels, they already have. It is precisely this "overwhelming multitude of stories and events" that makes each book so tantalizing. Both von Ziegesar and Williams-Garcia acknowledge that there cannot be only one story in a book about teenagers and New York City; the stories must be as intricate and intersecting as the city itself.

Things to Think About

1. With the exception of Jenny Humphrey, the characters in *Gossip Girl* and *Jumped* do not show much growth in their character development. How does this complicate the concept of the city as an ever-changing space?
2. How does conformity work as a through-line in *Gossip Girl* and *Jumped*? Do any of the characters choose to conform? Do any choose not to? What are they or aren't they conforming to? What are the implications of these choices?

Things to Explore

1. Almanzar, Belcalis and Klenord Raphael, songwriters. 2018. "Bodak Yellow." *Invasion of Privacy*. New York: Atlantic Records.
2. Brashares, Ann. 2017. *The Whole Thing Together*. New York: Delacorte Press.
3. Davis, Douglas, and Richard Walters, songwriters. 1986. "The Show." Doug E. Fresh. *Oh, My God!* Los Angeles: Reality Records.
4. Hardy, Jr., Nathaniel S., et al, songwriters. 1984. "Sucker M.C.'s." *Run-D.M.C.* New York: Profile Records.
5. Hunte, Angela, and Janet Sewell-Ulepic, with Shawn Carter and Alicia Keys. 2009. "Empire State of Mind." *The Blueprint 3*, New York: Roc Nation.
6. Jackson, Curtis, and Rob Tewlow, songwriters. 2003. "What Up Gangsta." *Get Rich or Die Trying*, New York: Shady Records.
7. McCarthy, Andy. "Class Act: Researching New York City Schools with Local History Collections." New York Public Library, October 20, 2014. https://www.nypl.org/blog/2014/10/20/researching-nyc-schools.

8. Goldsberry, Renee Elise, et al., songwriters. 2015. "The Schuyler Sisters." In *Hamilton: An American Musical*. New York: Atlantic Records.
9. Williams, Ismée. 2020. *This Train Is Being Held*. New York: Amulet.
10. Woodson, Jacqueline. 2010. *I Hadn't Meant to Tell You This*. New York: Puffin.
11. Zoboi, Ibi, ed. 2019. *Black Enough: Stories of Being Young and Black in America*. New York: Balzer + Bray.

References

Carroll, Jane Suzanne. 2014. "Catalysing Urban Interaction: Individual and Crowded Identities in New York City." In *Children's Literature and New York*, edited by Pádraic Whyte and Keith O'Sullivan, 97–110. New York: Routledge.

Fritz, Sonya Sawyer. 2014. "'New York is a Great Place': Urban Mobility in Twentieth-Century Children's Literature." In *Children's Literature and New York*, edited by Pádraic Whyte and Keith O'Sullivan, 85–96. New York: Routledge.

Halle, David, and Andrew A. Beveridge. 2011. "The Rise and Decline of the L.A. and New York Schools." In *The City, Revisited: Urban Theory from Chicago, Los Angeles, and New York*, edited by Dennis R. Judd and Dick Simpson, 137–68. Minneapolis: University of Minnesota Press.

Hine, Thomas. 1999. *The Rise & Fall of the American Teenager*. New York: Avon.

Judd, Dennis R., and Dick Simpson. 2011. *The City, Revisited: Urban Theory from Chicago, Los Angeles, and New York*. Minneapolis: University of Minnesota Press.

Maffi, Mario. 2004. *New York City: An Outsider's Inside View*. Columbus: The Ohio State University Press.

Pattee, Amy. 2006. "Commodities in Literature, Literature as Commodity: A Close Look at the Gossip Girl Series." *Children's Literature Association Quarterly* 31(2): 154–75.

Thabit, Walter, and Frances Fox Piven. 2003. *How East New York Became a Ghetto*. New York: New York University Press.

Turner, Sylvester (@SylvesterTurner). 2020. "As Mayor, I know that cities are ultimately made up of two things – people and places." Twitter, February 13. https://www.chicagomanualofstyle.org/tools_citationguide/citation-guide-2.html.

von Ziegesar, Cecily. 2002. *Gossip Girl*. Boston: Little, Brown.

Williams-Garcia, Rita. 2009. *Jumped*. New York: Amistad.

Young, Louise. 2013. *Beyond the Metropolis: Second Cities and Modern Life in Interwar Japan*. Berkeley: University of California Press.

CHAPTER ELEVEN

The Sensual City: Jason Reynolds's *When I Was the Greatest* and *The Boy in the Black Suit*

James F. Nicosia and Laura M. Nicosia

> *The impalpable sustenance of me from all things at all hours of the day, The simple, compact, well-join'd scheme, myself disintegrated, every one disintegrated yet part of the scheme . . .*
>
> —WALT WHITMAN, "CROSSING BROOKLYN FERRY"

THE DISCUSSION OF setting in secondary school literary studies often gets reduced to a fill-in-the-blank line on a postreading assessment. Indeed, in many texts offered to adolescents, setting serves as little more than an aside presented to inform student readers of the historicity of a "classic text" and thus quickly becomes an afterthought. Ask the average high school graduate exactly when and where *The Great Gatsby* takes place, and one is likely to receive a response of "East Egg," "West Egg" (without much sense of exactly where those places are or what makes them breathe as entities), and "the olden days of America." One of the most valuable assets of contemporary young adult literature, however, is that it takes place in "their time." One of the most valuable assets of literature of real cities is that it takes place in "their place." Considering most American students do live in the broad sense of the term *city*, it is exponentially important, then, that literature reads and breathes like the places they live and breathe in. As Hughes-Hassell and Guild (2002) say, "Today there are over 34 million teens living in urban areas and, just like the teens of 1967, these young adults want, and need, to see their lives represented in the literature they read" (35). To that end, contemporary realistic texts like those of Jason Reynolds, present a city that is vibrant and alive with sensual details that make setting as much as the subject of the novels as any other universal themes they present. Because of such interconnectedness of setting and theme, and because love and redemption prevail as themes, Reynolds subtly reaffirms the city as a place of love and redemption, as well, in his first two novels, *When I Was the Greatest* (2014) and *The Boy in the Black Suit* (2015). In short, the city is a place that nurtures its residents even as it presents unique challenges to them.

Reynolds's 2014 debut, *When I Was the Greatest,* opens with protagonist Allen (aka Ali) discussing with his best friend Noodles, "Would you rather live every day for the rest of your life with stinky breath, or lick the sidewalk for five minutes?" From that moment to the last page, where Ali reconciles his most important relationships after discovering that the city is better for being gray and imperfect, the novel exudes a love of storytelling, and as a result, every page exhibits a narrator absolutely engaged in the moment. And moments are what cities are all about; after all, at any given moment in any big city like Reynolds's Bedford-Stuyvesant Brooklyn, *something* is happening that is worth talking about. Hence, Ali always *has* something to talk about, even when, the reader soon realizes, not a lot of it is essential to driving a focused plot to its denouement and resolution.

The reader is integrated into Ali's Bed-Stuy not with a finite description, but with a book-long revelation of, and homage to, the city. It evolves as the story evolves, and as the characters evolve. The sense of place for the reader of Reynolds's stories, thus, is what Doreen Massey (2005) calls a "space as a simultaneity-of-stories so far" (9), and summarizes that the city is defined as a place wherein exists "collections of those stories, articulations within the wider power-geometries of space" (130). The city and its inhabitants are inextricable, and Reynolds lets his readers know this with his willingness to bring them into the mix from the first conversation to the last. Reynolds indeed recognizes, as Massey (2005) says, that "[a]rriving in a new place means joining up with, somehow linking into, the collection of interwoven stories of which that place is made" (119). Indeed, in *When I Was the Greatest*, stories *are* what the novel is all about; celebrating the city in its rich diversity is the underlying message of Reynolds—from the literary lineage of Walt Whitman via Langston Hughes—to his adolescent readers: you are alive, the place where you live is alive, so experience it, embrace it, celebrate it.

To establish a brief, but ongoing, understanding of what we mean when we even undertake to conceptualize cities, we begin with Linda McDowell's (1997) acknowledgment that "places are both concrete and symbolic. They are literally and metaphorically made up: of buildings, field systems, roads and railways as well as of myths and legends, statues and ceremonies that link people to a place" (2). In *When I Was the Greatest* (Roberts 2014), narrator Ali is unafraid to shine the light of his imagination upon Bed-Stuy. Massey and McDowell each suggest that to experience a place is to understand a place. When one participates in the stories shared by a narrator-in-the-know—the routines and ritual of waking, eating, visiting local establishments, and meeting local "regulars" in and around those establishments—one becomes a part of that community. Reynolds's Brooklyn is limned in just such a way, in both novels, so as to not merely acquaint the reader with the city and its populace but to incorporate the reader into the routines and rituals with its protagonists, Ali and Matt. As such, they "[join] up with, somehow linking into, the collection of interwoven stories of which that place is made" (Massey 2005, 119). This immersion in the narrative world, accelerated by Reynolds' abundant sensual details, brings the reader to a place where Georges Poulet (1970) says, "Whenever I read, I mentally pronounce an *I*, and yet the *I* which I pronounce is not myself" (60). Author and reader soon achieve a "common consciousness" (62). Such a transformation for a reader occurs in Reynolds's stories primarily as a result of the sensual immersion into the city.

The people and places of Reynolds's Bed-Stuy are presented more than merely as characters and backdrops, but rather they each are recognized as fascinating, thoughtfully integrated elements of the city with their own sensual qualities. When he does examine the local hangouts—even Knit Wit, the knitting store—he realizes that everything he knows about his mother, his father, his friends, his neighborhood, and the people are marvelously textured, flawed entities, not romantic tropes. As a result, this novel shows how subtle and profound moments of epiphany are in a teenager's life when he discovers the complexity of his city. This is a true coming-of-age novel. Not only does Ali learn about himself within the confines of family, but he also learns about his entire surroundings, and his place in it is both tenuous and inextricable. He *is* the city. As Tim Cresswell (2004) argues, "When humans invest meaning in a portion of space and then become attached to it in some way (naming is one such way) it becomes place" (10). Ultimately, Reynolds reaffirms the value of family, in whatever form it takes. But for Reynolds, *whatever form it takes* goes beyond immediate family, extended family, and friend groups. It includes everyone you might regularly run into in the city, for they all have names and they all have stories. And once each of their stories is told, the city is fleshed out for Ali, best friend Noodles, and the reader, and everyone is at least a little better off by the novel's end.

When I Was the Greatest

When the book opens, thoughtful and humorous narrator Ali thinks he knows everything about his world in Bed-Stuy Brooklyn. He lives in a modest apartment with his mother, little sister Jazz and friends Noodles and Needles next door. While his mother holds down two jobs, she does her best to be a concerned, loving parent, and her children respect her for that. As a result, they act as parental figures to each other and the essentially abandoned Noodles and Needles. But with a single mother holding down two jobs, Ali realizes something else important by the novel's end: it takes a village to raise a child, and many of the adults (and children) take on that responsibility, even when there are certainly elements who have abandoned that charge.

Because Noodles and Needles are left to their own devices, the plot takes form. Ali and Noodles get themselves invited to a block party that they probably shouldn't go to. Forced to bring the Tourette's-inflicted, constantly crocheting Needles along, the party turns violent when Needles says the wrong thing to the wrong person. The drama unfolds quickly from there, but this is a book to savor for its sensual details, not merely to "see what happens." As Massey (2005) recognizes in what she calls a place's "throwntogetherness" (141), the city's diverse citizens don't merely define or live in a place as they navigate their lives; they *produce* the city itself. Creswell (2004) navigates a different terminology when he says, "places are performed on a daily basis through people living their everyday life" (34), thus giving a more dynamic fluidity to a city. It is, to him and to Reynolds, an ever-evolving act, and each story-within-a-story contributes to that act.

At the novel's commencement in medias res, Ali and Noodles are engaging in a typical city-stoop game of Would You Rather, and this immediately immerses the reader in sensory details, albeit of the disgusting kind: licking the ground or having "shit breath, forever" (Reynolds 2014, 1). Let us not underestimate the power of the sound of words at the outset, with the boys engaged in realistic dialogue. Before Ali even gets to speak, we see Noodles's face as well: "He turned and looked at me with a huge grin on his face because he knew this was a tough one" (1). Then "he busted out laughing." Indeed, in Reynolds's debut, sound and vision are the preeminent sensory details that bring the reader into the city with the narrator Ali. Before the conversation is done, Ali professes to being "queasy" (another sensory detail).

Then a "sick black SUV came flying down the block. The stereo was blasting, but the music was all drowned out by the loud rattle of the bass, bumping, shaking the entire back of the truck" (1–2). In a lesser writer's hands, the vehicle would serve as foreshadowing for some later event; in a lesser editor's hands, it would have been stricken entirely. But the SUV serves an important purpose: it brings the sounds and sights of the city streets into the dialogue and into the reader's mind. But before it is overstated, Noodles slides right to his next entry of "Would you rather": "'Aight, aight, I got another one' . . . He shook his soda can to see if anything was left in it" (2). Again, Reynolds inserts specifics that serve no plot point or theme, but the sensory detail of shaking a soda can—an action everyone surely has done a myriad of times—brings the city, and Noodles, to life. Reynolds places his finger on the pulse of the city in one page, and he never takes it off as he masterfully inserts small but vital details such as these throughout.

Before chapter one is even halfway complete, Reynolds engages in another motif central to city stories, that of naming. Ali, we have already learned, was given his nickname by his sister as an ironic reference to the less-than-successful commencement of his boxing career. But Ali involves the reader in the story with his full-length retelling of the Noodles's and Needles's naming baptisms: "I bet you're wondering how he started getting called Noodles" (12). Ali indeed takes his time with this narrative, stopping to admit that "Noodles's nickname story is better than mine" (13), and it involves Jazz's secondhand extended visual narration relayed (as many city stories are) from the second-story window of their apartment. Little about this story serves major plot functions, but the establishment of the city viewed from the perspective of one's own home rings true. As Maffi (2004) says, "the act of seeing in New York (the act of seeing New York)—on the streets, beneath the towers, inside the houses, in the tunnels, on the bridges, inside the kaleidoscope—once again become a deeply emotional experience" (90). Readers understand inherently, even if they do not consciously consider it, that their view of their world literally is from the window of their home. Reynolds takes his time in delivering such details, to bring place to life for the reader. Without such details, his stories would be short, indeed, and would not be authentic paeans to Brooklyn, in particular, and the American city, in general.

The purpose here is not to analyze any one particular scene as quintessential to the novel. Indeed, for the city to thrive, it must have multiple hubs, all centered on the teller's vantage point. As Judd and Simpson (2011) warn, "[O]ne must acknowledge the limitation of any single storyline that proposes to interpret the 'urban'" (16). What Reynolds most excels at is constantly paying homage to the multiplicity of narratives in Ali's world. Where Ali is at any given moment when he relays a story of buying yarn, getting a haircut, going to a party, or hanging on his front stoop, Reynolds unhurriedly narrates the unique sensual details of the yarn store, the barber's home, the party's basement, the sidewalk and street outside his apartment. All have equal importance. As Maria Beville (2019) relates,

> [R]ather than merely existing as a physical place, the city is experience; individualised and multiplied in its alterity. While the city exists as a place to be read and is unique in every individual reading, it is also a place to be written, inspiring writers, artists, and thinkers to become lost in city streets and locales as they struggle to find new ways to meet the challenge of representing the unrepresentable. (1)

As such, this novel is about all the stories that Ali tells as much as the one that emerges as primary halfway through the novel.

That being said, if we were to arbitrarily choose one scene to examine in depth for the Whitmanian celebration of the most and least significant sensual details, one could do worse than observe chapter fifteen, wherein the loosely crocheted plot points achieve their denouement in a sacrificial act of love from Ali's wayward father. To do justice to the immediacy of the events, and their unhurried phenomenological unfolding, one would have to quote practically the entire chapter. "I woke up early the next morning," Ali begins, before correcting himself, "Well, I don't know if you can really call it waking up, since I never actually got to sleep" (Reynolds 2014, 200). He is in no more hurry now to skip what one might erroneously call unnecessary details than he was at any time in the novel. All is important, he has said, and he will not abandon that premise now.

As background, Needles's Tourette syndrome has accidentally gotten the boys in deep trouble, and John, Ali's father, has promised to remedy the situation. When Ali discovers a gun in John's car, however, he fears that the remedy will involve a violence that he, Ali, has repeatedly avoided—and he fears his father will either die over or be sent to jail for. Reynolds presents the reader with a barrage of immediate experiential details that would necessarily plague a boy like Ali, worried for his own safety and his father's. In a typical narrative, however, the following details would likely be glossed over. Not here. Instead, Ali takes the time to show his reader, almost in real time, that he

> rolled out of bed and hurried into the living room to see John. . . . It was important for me to see him, to talk to him, not that I could talk him out of it. I'm not even exactly sure that I wanted to. But just to see him and talk to him. You just never know, and I didn't want him leaving, and something happening, and me not catching him to say good-bye before he left. (200)

In less dynamic locales than the city, or even the city apartment, Ali's details might not be important to share, for in the rural, and even suburban, landscapes, destinations are more the goal. That is, in the latter locales, there are homes and central meeting places like malls, for example. Between them is what some call unconsidered space, traversed usually by car. Between "where I am" and "where I am going" is, conceptually, nothing. In the suburban landscape, for example, one might leave one's home, travel to pick up a friend, and then drive to the mall. Each of those three places is a destination. Everything in between does not matter, and indeed blurs, in the suburban landscape. In the rural landscape, typically, those destination places are even fewer and farther between. For the city, however, traversed as it is on foot, every step alters one's perspective and transports one into a new, vital place. As Carroll (2014) relates, "[T]there is no single clear path through the urban space, rather, the innumerable routes through the streets and paths intersect and diverge" (98). In the suburban and rural landscapes, the destination counts, not the journey. The in-between places serve as merely the conduit between *here* and *there*. In the city, the participant is always *here*, in a dynamic space.

Ali shifts from his visual and verbal details of the opening paragraph of chapter fifteen to auditory details in the next paragraph: "I hadn't heard any arguing or anything like that in the middle of the night, so I assumed it was cool with Doris for him to stay here," before providing scent-and-taste sensitivities, and more visual details: "When I came into the living room, the two of them were sitting on the couch having coffee. I couldn't believe my eyes" (Reynolds 2014, 200).

Sound enters the picture next, as each of the three awakened family members take their turns saying good morning. Then Reynolds shows his reader, once more at the pace of life, that Ali's mother, Doris, "stood up, gave me a kiss on the head, and then went to put her cup in the sink" (200–1). Out of context, it might be easy to read these words and question the quality of the writing, but that would be missing the point, indeed. One cannot take the events of the city out of context. All that happens in the city story is within context, whether the reader is immediately aware of this or not. The truth of the uninterrupted narrative reveals itself *as an uninterrupted narrative*, and the reader is immersed and engaged in each and every detail of a magnificent storyteller. In short, the reader not only does not mind the excruciating amount of sensual details, for the reader *is* immersed; one also does not bemoan the rich quality of one's first-hand experience, and Reynolds knows this. So the chapter rumbles along with a celebration of insignificant-but-vital details.

Evidence the scene between Ali's estranged-but-in-love parents as John prepares to leave and confront the man who has threatened his son:

> "And John," she started. She walked over to him. He stood up, and she wrapped her arms around him tight. She whispered something in his ear, and when she pulled away, she whipped toward to door so fast, I couldn't see her face. (201)

Once more, the sensual details available to Ali tell a so-much-richer story than the factual ones (perhaps: "My mother hugged my father.") ever could.

Ali and John engage in a dialogue of their own for a short while, wherein Ali is still assuming his father is resorting to violence, and as such, the reader believes so, as well. Then, poignantly, more sensual details:

> We sat quietly for a second, and then I got a whiff of coffee, and bacon, and cinnamon. I glanced over to the kitchen. No pots. No pans. Stove off.
>
> "Hey! Ma cooked for you?" I asked jealously. Doris never cooks breakfast for us because she leaves so early. If she had cooked breakfast for my father, I was going to be salty.
>
> John looked at me crazy and laughed. "Now, you know your mother ain't make no breakfast," he said, shaking his head. "I think it's Brenda upstairs. Go ahead up there and ask if you can have some."
>
> I laughed. "Ms. Brenda is cool, but she don't seem like the type to share food."
>
> John hooted. "Got that right!" (201)

It is a remarkable passage, yet one that is easy to overlook. Once more, in a lesser editor's hand, much of that scene might be deleted. Or perhaps, to assert a more romantic vision, this scene might have revealed Doris indeed as the cook. Instead, a tertiary character, Brenda, is brought into this vital scene, yet another reminder that the city is full of people, none of whom can ever conveniently disappear. The smell of food from the apartment upstairs will always remind you of the dynamics of the city. Furthermore, although the dialogue here may advance little, it does provide another insignificant but consequential element to the story: our relationships are formed as much by the small laughs we have about acquaintances as much as the big conversations about friends and family. In life, and especially city life, most of our conversations are small ones with acquaintances, and the most ironic touch is that because of this fact, they are as consequential to defining ourselves and performing the city as any others. As Ali himself says of this unrushed morning, "We didn't really talk about too much before he took off, or have any sort of amazing father/son lightbulb moment, but the time we spent, to me, was quality" (203).

The scene is already rich with detail, and it is scarcely three pages old. Ali, and the reader, may be anxiously awaiting the story's climax, but it is still "twenty minutes later" when John starts to leave (202). The actual leaving takes another page entirely, and then Ali returns to his second-floor window perspective: "Like usual, I walked over to the kitchen window to see him leave. There was really nothing to it. John just got into his car and pulled off. I leaned to the side to follow the car as far as I could, but before I knew it, it was gone" (203).

Much of what we have examined here could fall under the category of "There was really nothing to it," but while most of the details of Reynolds's narratives, and cities, can be called by this term, one must not mistake insignificant (literally, not signifying anything thematically or symbolically) for inconsequential (not changing one's life). Indeed, it is the insignificant—the sons of a prostitute who moves in next door; the needles a friend's mother gives a boy with Tourette's; the first meal a friend eats at your house, thus giving him the name Noodles—that often become the most consequential things in our urban lives.

The Boy in the Black Suit

Reynolds brings us another Brooklyn story that could speak for anyone from any number of American cities in *The Boy in the Black Suit* (2015). Matt is a 17-year-old from Bed-Stuy, Brooklyn, and his mother has just died from breast cancer. School has been in session for a few months, but getting back into the swing of things is impossible. All the usual high school drama is pointless to him now that he's seen more real drama up close.

Without his mother's income, Matt knows he has to get a job to help make ends meet. Rumor has it the Cluck Bucket fried chicken restaurant pays well, so he heads there to fill out an application. First, he meets a girl at the counter whom he later learns is named Love. Love's good looks are only matched by her maturity, sass, and strength. Maybe working here will be good. But then, halfway through the application, a vomiting episode occurs. Matt hates vomit. Maybe that offer to work with Mr. Ray, the funeral home director, might be a good idea after all. Matt takes out his only black suit—the one he wore to his mother's funeral—and it soon defines his identity as he seeks to find himself and overcome his overwhelming sense of loss by sharing others' losses at the funeral home.

One of the impressive things about Reynolds's characters is how they meet the realities of city life with such believable maturity. But there's a lot more—and a lot less—to this story, and Jason Reynolds's masterful limning of the city feels as much like memoir as it does fiction. It's loose and real, full of details that are superfluous yet telling. The accidental, the unimportant—that's what make up life in a city, and Reynolds transforms that which seems matter-of-fact into deep characterization and setting.

Against the backdrop of different funerals that Matt attends, Matt's father, drunk with depression, is hit by a car and forced to spend November and December in the hospital. Matt is going to have to make his way through the holidays on his own. Or maybe he won't. Reynolds is one of those writers who recognizes that adults do play a part in teens' lives, and Mr. Ray is a delightful character. Love, meanwhile, has a parallel story to Matt's, and their lives intertwine in ways that are more than simply mutual attraction. In his second novel, Reynolds again paints women as inspiring and intelligent, and his self-proclaimed "mama's boys" are all the richer for it.

Reynolds also excels at the sense of interiority that many boys this age have. With the world going on around them, boys often live so much in their own heads, out of step with their environment even as they are enmeshed in it: "Everyone was zipping by, bumping me, as I sort of floated through the halls like some kind of zombie" (Reynolds 2015, 2). Reynolds reveals that so well. He also writes love into each one of his relationships, and he does it in just the right amounts, too.

Like *When I Was the Greatest, The Boy in the Black Suit* is a study in character and place more than plot. This is a good thing, because Matt, Love, and Mr.

Ray command attention with every word they say, every thought they have, and the city and its smells (this is a novel rich in foods) jump off the page into the olfactory, auditory, and tactile senses.

Matt's experiences observing funerals from the back of the room function to illustrate to him various possibilities for his own path through grief. He has not really begun to address his own loss of his mother, so vicariously "attending" a variety of funerals allows him to try on different grief masks, if you will. He is often part of the group of attendees (even eating together with them at the subsequent repasts), but when the entire funeral process is completed, Matt is free to disconnect himself from the performance of grief and return to himself. Whether he realizes it or not, he changes and grows with each experience. As Carroll (2014) says, "The individual does not have to be subsumed by the crowd but . . . if a person can learn to become a crowd by themselves—that is to acquire or develop multiplicitous personae that reflect the multiplicity of the city—they can retain some control over their identity" (99). Matt dons his black suit and as such can blend in at the funerals as though he belongs, but when he takes the suit off, he becomes just another boy in Brooklyn.

When explaining to his best friend, Chris, why he works at a funeral home and attends other families' funerals, Matt thinks to himself:

> Of course, I couldn't tell him the truth. The truth that I was having a hard time telling myself. I *liked* the funerals. And in thinking about how I couldn't tell Chris that, I started thinking about why I was actually so into them in the first place. I wasn't just being a creep. Well, I sorta was, but it wasn't for no reason. I know that now. I liked watching other people deal with the loss of someone, not because I enjoyed seeing them in pain, but because, somehow, it made me feel better knowing that my pain isn't only mine. That my life isn't the only one that's missing something it will never have back. See? Reasons. (Reynolds 2015, 79)

Matt becomes one of a crowd—even when that crowd isn't part of his social network. He is subsumed by his own grief and shares the commonalities of grieving with (sometimes) complete strangers.

One of the more poignant, if insignificant, details of the early part of the narrative occurs when Matt considers his mother's recipe book, which she has left him. They had cooked together often, but since her death, even the consideration of the smells and tastes of his mother's food brought back too many sad memories from him, so he has avoided cooking since her death. In this passage, however, he is also sensitive to the visual stimuli of seeing her handwriting:

> [The book was] her way of passing the cooking torch so that I could do my thing in the kitchen without having to open up one of those lame, thick, usually way too girly cookbooks. . . . Written on the blue, nasty-stained cover was THE SECRET TO GETTING GIRLS, FOR MATTY, in my mother's loopy cursive. That was our joke, that cooking is what girls really like. Her telling me that definitely made me feel better about being a dude and knowing what a whisk and a colander are. That's for damn sure. . . .
>
> I tried to open it a few days before, but couldn't do it. Figured I'd give it another shot. I cracked it open, smack dab in the middle.
>
> THE OMG OMELETTE FOR MATTY (THANKS FOR TEACHING ME "OMG")
>
> Closed it. Immediately. Even though I was starving and that omelette—the OMG Omelette—would've hit the spot, I couldn't do it. Her writing, I could hear her voice. . . NO! (31)

This passage combines memory, touch, taste, sight, and sound in an overwhelming whirlwind of emotions. The passage is sad and wonderful at the same time, for Matt is unable to process all the emotions that the overabundant sensual details arouse in him.

Reynolds, in this novel quite divergent from his debut, does not divest himself of the major considerations of identity, performance, and the city as they reveal themselves in sensuality. In fact, the gustatory senses are particularly heightened in this book, in both positive and negative ways. Evidence the following scene where Matt meets his eventual love interest, Love, at the Cluck Bucket restaurant:

> [T]he door swung open and a young girl came rushing in, her hand pressed tight to her mouth, her cheeks bulging from her face. And before she could get to the bathroom—hell, before she could even get all the way inside—she spewed red, lumpy slime all over the already sticky floor. It looked like that old-lady pudding. What's it called? Tapioca? Yeah. It was like tapioca. But red. . . . Everything about throw-up is gross. The way it looks, the way it smells, the way it sounds. All of it. Straight-up nasty. (14)

The scent is so powerful (indeed, is it not in real life?) that Matt can no longer consider working there. Would the reader have accepted Matt's taking a job there, either?

But scents are also comforting when they are familiar smells of places we associate with intimate memories. Evidence the dynamic smells and visions of the local bodega run by the Pakistani man known as Jimmy, a place Matt associates with fond gustatory memories of his father:

> I stepped into the store and was greeted by the rank smell of cat litter and cooked cold-cut meat. . . . "Let me get honey-glazed on a roll. Lettuce, tomato, mayo, provolone, sweet peppers, oil and vinegar, black pepper, meat and cheese, hot," I rattled off like naming brothers and sisters I don't have. I've been ordering the same sandwich since I was a kid. It's the way my dad orders." (33, 34)

The food is associated with metaphoric siblings in this passage, and it is a fleshing-out of the familiar. In a more predictable writer's hands, the reader might expect some grand climax to occur in the bodega, for it is so lovingly, carefully crafted by Reynolds through his sensitive narrator Matt's descriptions. But once again, the reader quickly learns that large and small are immaterial in the city, for wherever one is, with whomever one is conversing, becomes central at the moment of indulgence. Unlike Chekhov's gun principle, which requires every element mentioned in a literary work be utilized later in that work (Goldberg, 1976, 163; Rayfield, 1997, 203; Simmons, 1962, 190), Reynolds's small moments of sensuality and memory are not foreshadowing a climactic event, but they are notes in an epiphanic symphony.

Finally, as Matt begins to fall for Love, he is able to consider what is for him, the strongest sensations: taste and smell. He recalls his mother's statements about the way to a girl's heart being through her stomach: "I also hoped she was right about, y'know, cooking being a way to get girls" (Reynolds 2015, 172). And he is ready to confront her recipe book, finally, with the hope of impressing Love on their first date:

> That gave me about two hours now to make the cookies. I broke out the sifter, the mixing bowl, the mixer, some measuring cups, and the old wooden spoon my mother loved to use. Then, finally, I opened up the notebook—THE SECRET TO GETTING GIRLS, FOR MATTY—and flipped through until I found the recipe. . . .
>
> I could actually hear my mom's voice while reading the recipe. (169–70)

The sensual description of creating chocolate chip cookies culminates in Matt's newfound willingness to hear his mother's voice. While this saddens him, it allows him to process the myriad emotions he has about moving forward in his life, allowing new people in his life, and confronting his feelings about his mother's death. Although the theme of confronting familial death certainly is not confined to the urban environment, in a Reynolds's penned Bed-Stuy portrait, the insignificant but essential details that bombard the protagonist lead to his epiphany. Only in the city will one find a Pakistani-owned bodega in a black neighborhood across the street from an African American–owned funeral home serving franchised fried chicken at a repast for recently deceased families of every imaginable diversity. All those details are vital for Matt's healing.

If, as Jane Suzanne Carroll (2014) says, "landscape and identity are inextricably connected" (97), Jason Reynolds's Ali and Matt in *When I Was the Greatest* (2014) and *The Boy in the Black Suit* (2015), respectively, define themselves as they tell their multiple stories of the city and vice versa. Furthermore, the reader who identifies with either the protagonists or the city also defines themself and their place along with these protagonists. Such a journey for the reader can only occur with full immersion not only in the characters and events of the book but the place, as well. That is where Jason Reynolds has excelled from his first novels onward and where his readers will find much to celebrate.

In the Classrooms

Ebony Elizabeth Thomas (2011) argues that, as readers become immersed in and indoctrinated into urban literary landscapes, this "contribute[s] to the formation of [their] identities, as well as their sense of being anchored in worlds both fictional and real" (13). Using that quotation as a departure point, any number of pre-, during, and postreading activities can be constructed by a teacher sensitive to bringing awareness to their students of the sensual details of Reynolds's city, and their own.

Many of Jason Reynolds's texts lend themselves to easy implementation in the classroom, not merely as texts to contemplate, but as creative writing exemplars, personal-response considerations, and philosophical engagements. Students may be asked to read a particular scene—any of the aforementioned vignettes would serve nicely—and take notes on the sensual details. Those in urban environments may be asked to create a comparable text for their own city, using such a scene as a model. Middle and secondary school students can use this opportunity to sensitize themselves to their own environment, which will encourage them to not only observe their community more closely but also to see how they, themselves, participate in the performance of that community as someone who lives, goes to school, and plays in that community. In a creative writing classroom, on this and collegiate levels, writing stories of one's own favorite (and/or least favorite) locations in town can help writers bring to life the details of everyday existence as Reynolds so masterfully does. Writers on all levels struggle to "show, not tell," and using his work as a model will find writers more facilely understanding the illustrative responsibility and creating their own vivid settings.

For personal response narratives, students can be encouraged to make comparisons between the place they shop for groceries, for example, and Jimmy's bodega in *The Boy in the Black Suit* (Roberts 2015). Similarly, the recipes that play so largely, and present so many scent-and-taste details in that novel can serve as comparative pieces for students to share their own experiences with "Grandma's cookies" or "Dad's pot roast." Whether students have complete familiarity with the foods of Reynolds's Brooklyn, or none at all, food is a universal theme (some would say a universal good), and most cultures revere their cooking traditions. Holding up one's own food indulgences to those of

Matt's mother can help shape an understanding of the unifying qualities of food, even when specifics of those foods may differ widely. The key to all these assignments is recognition and discussion of the sensual details that Reynolds himself presents and the subsequent encouragement (perhaps requirement, for those students who need concrete direction) of utilizing all five senses in a one-, two-, or ten-page re-creation of a place or food in their lives.

Higher-level courses (although we contend that *most* classrooms can engage in esoteric, high-level theoretical considerations) may engage students in the metacognitive implications of the performative nature of a city. This may be particularly effective if the students in the classroom do come from an urban, or even suburban, environment (although we would not have a difficult time being convinced that the following concepts might apply to a rural town, as well). Students in high schools often take part in the performative nature of their schools, for example, especially when engaging in sports or academic competitions.

Students can be asked to argue that they are their city and vice versa. They might be asked to identify perhaps three places in which they take part in regular activities (of any nature). They also would be asked to consider what other people participate in the same (or alternate!) activities there and how this might connect two disparate people in a community of sorts. We have had one student write a compelling essay on how her dance class empowered her as a person who had previously considered herself unathletic. The essay went on to consider how she would regularly see a boy coming into the building on Saturdays for martial arts class, as the building was used for multiple purposes. For the longest time, she relayed, she did not pay attention to or consider the boy or anyone else who came to the class that followed her dance lesson. But as time went on, she would begin to nod, say hello, and take part in short conversations with the boy. To summarize an engagingly long story, they subsequently became friends, and, ultimately, she realized, place was vital to her understanding of herself, and her relationships were formed as a result of a city storefront gym. Connections are made in such environments as cities, where a range of people traverse and transact, intersect and commingle. As such, identity is also a consideration of such an assignment: personal identity, communal identity (people who share experiences), and community identity (the more we take part in activities in the same place, the more this defines our city).

Things to Think About

1. **Gentrification in Bed Stuy.** This video presents the opinions of long-time residents of Bed-Stuy Brooklyn about the gentrification of their city in the twenty-first century: https://www.youtube.com/watch?v=B6uF57gSqFk.
2. **Jason Reynolds | Brooklyn Is Masquerading as The World | Ep. 11.** Fascinating video of Jason Reynolds sharing his thoughts about Brooklyn with no holds barred. Discusses racist concerns in a thoughtful, honest way: https://www.youtube.com/watch?v=u175oc5BM8w.
3. **Jason Reynolds: "Write. Right. Rite.": Create an Award for Yourself.** Jason Reynolds, recently named National Ambassador for Young People's Literature, encourages young people to write and says, "Create an award for yourself." Quietly inspirational and thoroughly encouraging: https://www.youtube.com/watch?v=ZOLaHL7tlTc.

Things to Explore

1. **Bed-Stuy Brooklyn. Block-by-block.** A *New York Times* video recording of the Bedford-Stuyvesant section of Brooklyn, bringing to life in a visual way the Brooklyn of Jason Reynolds's stories. This would be both an excellent prereading or postreading activity, depending on student schemata. One might bring to light setting before reading the book, if a teacher believed students needed to "see" the place before engaging in Reynolds's stories, but this would also serve to confirm students' own sense of place if shown afterward and asked to compare what they see in the video with what they saw in their head as they read Reynolds's novel. https://www.

nytimes.com/2015/01/22/realestate/block-by-block-bed-stuy-brooklyn-video-series.html.

2. **Walking Tour of Bedford-Stuyvesant, Brooklyn, NYC.** The same could be done for this video, which shows an individual exiting a subway and literally walking the streets. It does not have the same production qualities of the *Times* video, but it moves slowly enough for the watcher to take in the setting. That being said, very little happens in this video, so a sense of dynamism might be missing from this, in some minds. https://www.youtube.com/watch?v=Cwq3iLYgkSk.
3. **A Conversation with Walter Dean Myers.** A full-length interview with Reynolds's inspiration and mentor, Walter Dean Myers, one of the first black writers of young people's literature to be recognized and celebrated in America. https://www.youtube.com/watch?v=SyWD6PemQMM.

References

Beville, Maria. 2019. "Introduction: Otherness and the Urban." *Otherness: Essays & Studies* 7(1). http://www.otherness.dk/journal/otherness-essays-studies-71/.

Carroll, Jane Suzanne. 2014. "Catalysing Urban Interaction: Individual and Crowded Identities in New York City." In *Children's Literature and New York*, edited by Pádraic Whyte and Keith O'Sullivan, 97–110. New York: Routledge.

Cresswell, Tim. 2004. *Place: A Short Introduction*. Malden, MA: Blackwell.

Goldberg, Leah. 1976. *Russian Literature in the 19th Century: Essays*. Jerusalem: Magnes Press, Hebrew University.

Hughes-Hassell, Sandra, and Sandy L. Guild. 2002. "The Urban Experience in Recent Young Adult Novels." *The ALAN Review* 29(3): 35–39.

Judd, Dennis R., and Dick Simpson, eds. 2011. *The City, Revisited: Urban Theory from Chicago, Los Angeles, and New York*. Minneapolis: University of Minnesota Press.

Maffi, Mario. 2004. *New York City: An Outsider's Inside View*. Columbus: The Ohio State University Press.

Massey, Doreen. 2005. *For Space*. Thousand Oaks, CA: Sage Publications.

McDowell, Linda. 1997. "Introduction: Rethinking Place." In *Undoing Place?: A Geographical Reader*, edited by Linda McDowell, 1–12. New York: Routledge.

Poulet, Georges. 1970. "Criticism and the Experience of Interiority." *The Structuralist Controversy: The Languages of Criticism and the Sciences of Man*, edited by Richard Macksey and Eugenio Donato, 56–72. Baltimore: Johns Hopkins University Press.

Rayfield, Donald. 1997. *Anton Chekhov: A Life*, New York: Henry Holt and Company.

Reynolds, Jason. 2014. *When I Was the Greatest*. New York: Antheneum.

Reynolds, Jason. 2015. *The Boy in the Black Suit*. New York: Antheneum.

Simmons, Ernest J. 1962. *Chekhov: A Biography*, Chicago: University of Chicago Press.

Thomas, Ebony Elizabeth. 2011. "Landscapes of City and Self: Place and Identity in Urban Young Adult Literature." *The ALAN Review* 38(2): 13–22.

CHAPTER TWELVE

An Author's Perspective: Music Lives in the City

Mary Rand Hess

THE CITY IS like a rock band or a jazz orchestra—it's rhythm and harmony and, on a sweet day, pure melody. Music is movement, and so are the city and her people. The cadence of diverse voices: sopranos, altos, tenors, baritones . . . mixed in with car horns, hissing busses, bicycle bells, radios buzzing, street musicians belting out tales, skateboards flying, the roaring of airplanes overhead, collective shoes (of every style) pounding the pavement, the whistling of breaks and momentum coming to a halt, all contribute to the city's great and powerful symphony.

Then there's the laughter, shouting, bantering, whispering, and humming caught up in the air, while doors open and close to the faces of people walking to the beat of their own agendas, walking toward their singular and collective fates. All of it brings about an unmistakable magic. This is any given day, in any given city around the world, where so much happens in a single pulse. Yet each city is like a person, unique with culture and personality. But cities all share something in common . . . they never fall silent. There is always music living there, even in our fictional stories that take place in urban settings.

When Kwame Alexander and I set out to write our young adult novel in verse, *Solo* (Alexander and Hess 2017), we wanted to capture the musical essence of cities: Hollywood and the greater Los Angeles area, and Accra, the capital city of Ghana (along with the important rural setting of the music-filled village of Konko). We wanted to write an ode to self-identity, love, family, forgiveness, redemption, culture, community, and the edgy, beautiful, complex history of rock and roll that is the playlist of our main character, Blade's life.

Blade is a musician in his own right, and the only thing he has in common with his rock-and-roll legend father is the music that lives inside of them, the rock tunes that color their city and world. In Blade's troubles, it is a wandering musician named Robert who gives him perspective and understanding, while encouraging Blade to find his truth. Street musicians are kind of mythic like that. What are their stories? How do they appear, then disappear the next time you step on the same city street or pier? Were they there to give you some kind of sign? To sing or play a song as medicine for your soul? Some of the most gifted musicians in the world perform on urban streets, but they remain rather anonymous (to an extent). We wanted Robert to have that mysterious quality, as one of Blade's angels in a city that wants to swallow him whole. And it is the music that connects these two friends in their brief but memorable exchanges. One is rich and famous by default, the other obscure and humble, and yet both live and breathe music in and around Hollywood. To Blade, Robert seems to hold the secret keys to the city and life in general:

> I walk
> the boardwalk
> looking for Robert,
> a magician
> who turns worries
> into songs.
>
> In between gigs
> he sits
> under a
> palm tree, smiling
> with the few teeth
> he's still got.
>
> Tourists leave
> green

in his black trumpet case,
while he
melts the *blues,*
bending the notes
like a storytelling machine,
and wailing
like the music's
gonna save him,
and us too
if we're lucky. (78)[1]

I think most people can relate to taking a moment to pause, to feel the pulse of live music, to relish in its mystery, and to erase the pain and worry of an uncertain world.

Kwame and I wanted Blade to travel across the globe to find a new perspective and to face the questions that haunt him, to land in a different place with new possibilities. So we decided to surprise him with a long-held family secret, forcing Blade to travel across time zones to Ghana. When he lands in Accra, the sights and sounds, the chords of the city, are there to greet him in full, sweltering heat. When he steps off the plane, he is welcomed by the nuances of a vibrant, high-energy, and loud city. We wanted Blade, and, in essence, our readers, to feel the similarities and differences between Hollywood and Accra:

Outside
of the airport
in Accra,
what hits me faster
and harder
than the torrid sun
are the loud
taxi drivers
boiling
in anger
who try
to seize
my suitcase
while arguing

like boxers
in a ring.

Lucky me,
I choose the taxi driver
with no AC
who listens
to Garth Brooks. (219)

For further perspective, we had Blade leave Accra for an awakening experience in the rural village of Konko. On his way there, as he leaves the city, he passes the familiar and the unfamiliar on his journey to find himself:

On the way to the village, we pass
gas stations
and malls
and condos
and fancy cars
and junksters
and traffic lights
and traffic
and car horns
and road rage
and more traffic
and homeless
and women
carrying kids
on their backs
and tubs
on their heads
filled with
plantain chips,
coat hangers,
pillows, and
everything
you could possibly
ever need
to buy. (220)

You can feel the musical notes in the vivid city scenes, hear the street noise that Blade hears, and imagine a world that's as alive as a rock concert. All Blade has to do now is let the music find him.

It is bliss to hear music read from a book. It brings rich and unique settings to life for the writer and the reader. Music is how ideas and culture are expressed; it is the vibe and vibrancy that calls people together in every place. It's electricity that sweeps through metropolitan life and the energy that never stops sparking an impromptu symphony of sounds. Cities hold the stories of rock stars, rap artists, and jazz greats who walked the streets before us, against the backdrop of authentic, fictional characters living out their own journeys, as real as the places that inspired them to come to life. And music will always be there for us . . . on every street corner, in all types of venues, in parks, on piers, on the stage, in countless cities across the world, and on the page.

Note

1. All lyric excerpts taken from *Solo* by Kwame Alexander with Mary Rand Hess Copyright ©2017 by Kwame Alexander. Used by permission of Blink YA Books.

Reference

Alexander, Kwame, and Mary Rand Hess. 2017. *Solo*. Grand Rapids, MI: Blink YA Books.

CHAPTER THIRTEEN

Visions of the City: Examining Urban Landscapes in Shaun Tan's Visual Narratives

Wendy R. Williams and Kristina D. ByBee

Shaun Tan's stories capture the strangeness, excitement, and loneliness of urban life. His complex visual landscapes in *The Arrival* (2006), *The Red Tree* (2011b),[1] *Cicada* (2019), and *Tales from the Inner City* (2018) have wonderful potential in education for challenging and expanding students' understandings of cities. The settings in these works are simultaneously fantastic and familiar, inspiring wonder in readers of all ages. This chapter introduces readers to Shaun Tan, highlights a selection of his works, and offers teaching suggestions for secondary classes.

A Biographical Introduction to Shaun Tan

Shaun Tan is an artist and writer who grew up in Perth, Australia. He describes his mother as "Anglo-Australian" and his father as "Malaysian Chinese" (Tan 2011a, 7). He has written of his childhood that "[a]t that time and place, being half-Chinese was unusual and cause enough to feel like an outsider" (Tan 2011a,

7). Many of Shaun Tan's visual narratives deal with the theme of fitting in. He worked on concept art for the film *Wall-E* (Stanton 2008) and won an Academy Award in 2010 for his short film *The Lost Thing* (Ruhemann and Tan 2010). Some of Tan's picturebooks[2] include *The Rabbits* (2011b, illustrator), *The Lost Thing* (Tan 2011b), *The Red Tree* (2011b), *Rules of Summer* (2014), and *Cicada* (2019), and his volumes of short stories include *Tales from Outer Suburbia* (2008), *Tales from the Inner City* (2018), and *The Singing Bones* (2015, based on the Grimm brothers' fairy tales). Tan has also produced one longer work that defies classification, *The Arrival* (2006), and he has published a collection of his drawings in *The Bird King: An Artist's Notebook* (2010).

This artist has suggested that creativity is about "squinting at the archive of experience from new angles" (Tan 2001a, 9), and he describes his art style as existing "somewhere in between the world of fine art and science fiction" (Davidson 2010, 40). Many of his books deal with serious themes, such as isolation, depression, colonization, immigration, inequality, and sustainability. However, he has found that young children are able to "grasp the hidden optimism that adults sometimes miss . . . [and] to find positive linings in grim stories" (Tan 2016, 38–39). Tan points out that picturebooks are not just for kids: "There is no reason why a 32-page illustrated story can't have equal appeal for teenagers or adults as they do for children. After all, other visual media such as film, television, painting or sculpture do not suffer from narrow preconceptions of audience" (Tan 2001b, 4–5).

A Selection of Shaun Tan's Works

Shaun Tan's books contain unique depictions of urban life. In the following sections, we discuss *The Arrival* (2006), *The Red Tree* (2011b), *Cicada* (2019), and *Tales from the Inner City* (2018), which could be used in a variety of ways in secondary education.

The Arrival

The Arrival (Tan 2006) is a 128-page visual narrative that is printed on large sheets of paper. Most would consider it a graphic novel or picturebook. The sepia and black-and-white tones, frames/borders, and cover suggest that this story is a photo album, yet the book makes use of film techniques as well (e.g., flashbacks, establishing shots, close-ups, high/low angles, lighting, blurring). *The Arrival*'s most striking feature, however, is the absence of words, which forces readers to stumble through this new land, experiencing it like the protagonist in the story, an immigrant in a strange new world. "Without using language, this [book] conveys what it is like to be a stranger who has just arrived, not knowing the language or the customs of a foreign land" (Williams and Blasingame 2017, 245). The city where the protagonist lands—dropped there by a box tied to a balloon after he is processed through immigration—is many things to the immigrants who end up there: a large, bustling, exciting center of life; a land of opportunity; a confusing place that challenges newcomers to learn its language, rules, and customs; and a diverse world where people connect and share memories of places they left behind. The city also impacts the main character in important ways: he wonders at it, is challenged by it, and learns how to navigate his way through it. Ultimately, he makes the place his home. Photographs of Ellis Island inspired this book ("Shaun Tan Interview" n.d.), yet the world in *The Arrival* is something else altogether, with its fantastical creatures, buildings, and machines. Students will be surprised by the book's wordless format, the strangeness of the cities portrayed, and that such a powerful story can be conveyed through images alone.

The Red Tree

The Red Tree, which appears in *Lost and Found* (Tan 2011b), is a picturebook about depression. It begins, "Sometimes the day begins with nothing to look forward to / and things go from bad to worse / darkness overcomes you" (n.p.). The images in this book depict a protagonist who wanders around in dreamlike settings. In one image, she is trapped in a bottle on a beach. In another, she waits on top of a gigantic snail, whose shell she is etching lines into as if keeping track of time. However, at the end of this story, the protagonist returns to her room to find a bright red plant sprouting, and then blossoming, into a beautiful tree. The text reads, "Suddenly there it is right in front of you bright and vivid" (n.p.). Careful viewers will notice that every page of this picturebook contains one red leaf from this plant as if signifying a glimmer of hope even when all appears lost. Much of the story consists of the protagonist in dreamlike landscapes, but there are also pages depicting the city where she lives. In this urban landscape, the main character appears small and insignificant. In fact, her surroundings seem to reflect her inner world and feelings. Although *The Red Tree* deals with depression, it is ultimately a hopeful book and one that secondary readers, in particular, will relate to.

Cicada

Cicada (Tan 2019) is a picturebook about a working cicada's bleak world. The first page of the text reads, "Cicada work in tall building. Data entry clerk. Seventeen year. No sick day. No mistake. Tok Tok Tok!" (n.p.). As the story progresses, readers learn that the character is not eligible for a promotion because "human resources say cicada not human" (n.p.). He must go twelve blocks away to use the restroom, and he loses pay for this. Despite the cicada's hard work, he is mistreated and bullied. One image shows the cicada on the floor and a coworker's foot squishing him (like a bug). When he retires, no one seems to care. Climbing the staircase to the top of the building, he reflects on the fact that he no longer has a job, funding, or anywhere to live (he had been living in a closet at work). "Time to say goodbye" (n.p.), the text ominously reads. On the edge of the roof, he suddenly sheds his skin, and a red cicada emerges, flying off to freedom, joining others. In this story, the gray urban world where the cicada works is oppressive. It is only by flying away to return to nature that he is truly free. (An alternative reading could be that he has died rather than shed his skin.) Like *The Arrival*, this is an immigrant story, yet it does not shy away from depicting the racism and inequality that immigrants may encounter in their new land. Although this book presents readers with a negative view of urban life, it does so in visually striking ways. It also exposes the artificiality of urban constructions and norms, which is worth addressing in a larger study of representations of urban cities. *Cicada* does deal with mature topics; however, like *The Red Tree*, this book ends on a hopeful note. It is sure to provoke discussions about where students feel at home (or not), what they envision for their own future careers, and how people should treat each other.

Tales from the Inner City

Tales from the Inner City (Tan 2018) is a collection of twenty-five illustrated stories set in an urban area, each focusing on a different animal. The stories are connected through their setting in an unnamed city rather than being linked by plot. A story about a missing cat reveals that strangers in a large urban area share more in common than they think. A story about sky fishing from a roof is magical and tragic. In the stories where animals are depicted in human situations and spaces (e.g., boardroom, airport), the familiar is made strange, and the notion that urban structures and behaviors are inevitable and normal is disrupted. This volume questions and complicates assumptions about urban life. What if your neighbors thought your cat was really their cat? What if there were horses running freely in the city, but they could only be seen through the innocent, imaginative eyes of toddlers? What if an entire species (bears, in one tale) filed a lawsuit against humans for the destruction of their species? Maybe, just maybe, humans should consider the millions of birds, fish, insects, and mammals that exist in the urban spaces that we have come to think of as places for humans. In this book, Tan disrupts the long-standing notion that humans control urban spaces. The beautiful illustrations can be described as realism meets surrealism: orcas float in the sky; bears climb courthouse stairs; rhinos block freeway traffic. Secondary students living in urban environments will identify with many of Tan's renderings of city settings: the ubiquitous skyscraper with floor-to-ceiling windows, multistory apartment buildings with fire escapes, and the port city pier where fishing boats bring in the day's catch. This is a book that will get students talking.

Shaun Tan in the Classroom

Teachers of all levels are using Shaun Tan's works in the classroom for a range of purposes. For example, Tan's books have been used to explore the impact of images versus words (Reid and Dyer 2018, 54), the possibilities of a picturebook versus a film (Dallacqua et al. 2015, 213–14), and powerful themes such as immigration (Rhoades et al. 2015, 322). In this section, we offer three additional teaching suggestions for using Shaun Tan's works with secondary students: (1)

the urban environment research project, (2) visual analysis, and (3) creative and personal writing.

Urban Environment Research Project

Tales from the Inner City (Tan 2018) could be used to launch an urban environment research project, an assignment that weaves together research, narrative, and images in a digital format. Vasudevan (2010) posits such projects can be especially empowering in an era of high stakes testing, "as youth are seeking new spaces for communication and composing, accessing a wide range of information sources, seeking and finding new audiences for their words and works" (43). Multimodal projects give students the opportunity to compose and construct "new kinds of texts" (47) that combine student narrative and images with research.

Teachers may want to introduce news articles or other media detailing credible stories of wild animals in the city. For example, in July 2019, Chicagoans escaping the heat of summer at Humboldt Park noticed an unusual creature swimming in the lagoon: a 5-foot-long alligator (Chappell 2019). The news of an alligator in urban Chicago quickly moved from a local story to national news. Americans took to social media to discuss, debate, and, naturally, offer potential names for the city's newest celebrity. Another option for teachers is to connect students to websites about animal conservation projects. For example, the "Urban Fishing Cat Conservation Project" describes a movement to save a nocturnal wild cat in Colombo, Sri Lanka (see item 4 in "Things to Explore").

Reading Tan's (2018) *Tales from the Inner City* invites essential questions about how animals have adapted to the cities humans have constructed and how humans and animals should exist together in city spaces. Students could list all of the animals they encounter on a typical day in their community. They could also consider several questions:

- Which animals exist in the urban environment because humans brought them there (i.e., pets), and which animals are native to the area?
- What animals were once native and/or numerous in your community?

- How are humans and animals coexisting in both negative and positive ways in the urban landscape?
- Are there conservation projects seeking to protect particular animals in your community?

Students could explore these questions in groups or individually. After conducting research about animals in the city, students could use their phones to take digital photographs and videos of animals in their community, claiming agency as they craft their own stories of humans and animals in urban settings. This information could then be synthesized into an urban environment research report. This digital project allows students to make real-world connections to *Tales from the Inner City* and examine their own place in their communities.

Visual Analysis

Another strategy we recommend is to use visual analysis with Shaun Tan's works. This can help secondary students delve deeper into the cities he portrays in his books. After all, Shaun Tan's illustrations demand that readers look closely in order to pick up on clues and make meaning. According to the New London Group (1996), when working with multimodal texts—that is, compositions that are made up of many modes (e.g., visual, linguistic, spatial, gestural, auditory)—it is helpful for readers/viewers to have access to metalanguage, "a language for talking about language, images, texts, and meaning-making interactions" (77). For Tan's works, students will benefit from exploring visual concepts such as color, shape, line, position, borders, and symbols. There are many fantastic resources to support teachers and students in acquiring visual vocabulary, most notably Frank Serafini's (2014) *Reading the Visual*. Furthermore, Scott McCloud's (1993) *Understanding Comics*, Will Eisner's (2008) *Graphic Storytelling and Visual Narrative*, and Molly Bang's (2016) *Picture This* are useful for exploring how visual design impacts storytelling. It would also benefit students to learn about basic film concepts, especially shots, angles, and lighting. The Columbia Film Language Glossary is an excellent online resource (see "Things to Explore").

The Arrival (Tan 2006) contains striking depictions of multiple cities, and each image employs design elements to convey information. For example, chapter one provides a view of the city the protagonist is leaving behind. While the rows of buildings are relatively light, there is a dark, menacing force taking over the streets. The triangular spikes on this creature (or creatures) suggest danger. The family appears tiny by comparison, and this use of size and scale communicates that they are less powerful than the force that surrounds and hovers above them. A high angle, looking down at this family, hints at their vulnerability. In chapter two of *The Arrival*, the protagonist arrives at a new land by boat. There are two rounded statues leaning in toward each other, shaking hands, suggesting that this land is welcoming to immigrants. The rounded shapes and lines, the use of symmetry, and brighter lighting create a sense of wonder and comfort. However, in a terrifying image in chapter three, a character has a flashback about the city he left behind. Readers see giant figures chasing people down as they run through the city. The Dutch (tilted) angle, diagonal lines, and use of size and scale communicate danger. Students will enjoy exploring the different representations of cities in this book, as there is so much to discover.

Of note, Maureen Bakis (2012) uses only chapter one of *The Arrival* (Tan 2006) with students. She has students examine the cover of the book, read the first chapter, and write in response to prompts, including "Describe the mood of the piece. What specific aspects of the visual images contribute to the mood?" (35). In fact, her journal questions could be modified to focus on the cities portrayed in *The Arrival*. Students could comment on how inviting each city is (or is not) and point to the specific visual elements and design choices that convey that information. Students could also compare the cities within the book.

Although *The Red Tree* (in Tan 2011b) mostly consists of dreamlike backgrounds, there are a few places where readers see the urban world in which the protagonist lives. A few pages into the story, she is walking down a street next to a five-story building that looks to be residential. There are several other people near her, but they are going their own ways and not looking at each other. No one seems to notice the enormous fish hovering above her, a symbol of her depression. Her bright orange hair creates salience, helping viewers know exactly where on the page to find her. Everything else on this page is a variation of brown or gray to reinforce the sad mood. A couple of pages later, the protagonist is at the foot of an incredibly steep staircase. Other people are walking to the left or right, all depicted in profile. They are slumped forward and not interacting. These characters seem small in comparison to the space. The gray tones and industrial furnaces add to this strangeness of this scene. Later in the story, the protagonist is walking on a lifted path that winds alongside chimney tops. A menacing creature that is made out of metal can be seen in the background. This dark figure has sharp fingers and a black tail, creating a contrast with the white sidewalk the protagonist is walking on and the large white dice she holds. Based on the number of structures crammed into this frame, this city must have a large population, yet no other people can be seen.

In *Cicada* (Tan 2019), the grays of the city and the skyscraper where the protagonist works convey the emotional coldness of this environment. At the beginning of this book, the end pages are dull gray geometric shapes, depicting the monotony of the cityscape. At the end of the book, however, the end pages are colorful and wild, depicting nature. Readers will immediately notice how few colors are used in this book. Almost everything viewers can see inside this skyscraper is a shade of gray: cubicles, elevator doors, furniture, staircases, and characters' clothing. Outside, even the sky is gray. However, the elevator button lights are green, as are the cicada's head, hands, badge, and a leaf he eats. The use of green creates salience, drawing viewers' eyes to anything with life in it: the protagonist, a potential way out, and natural food. At the end of the story, when the cicada sheds its skin, it emerges as a red cicada with wings. Soon the gray sky is filled with dozens of these red creatures. In addition to the use of color in the book, several other visual devices are employed. For example, high angles are used when the protagonist climbs the stairs and when colleagues are abusing him. The design choice to move the perspective up high, so that viewers have to look down at the protagonist, visually communicates the character's vulnerability. Another interesting design choice in this book is office cubicles appear to stretch beyond the page in every direction. This repetition creates a chilling effect, as the pattern seems to have no end.

Having access to a wide range of visual concepts enables secondary students to use precise language to describe what they see. Familiarity with these concepts also provides students with structures for thinking about how design choices impact the storytelling. When students are asked to conduct a visual analysis of images in Shaun Tan's books, they must pause and look closely, noticing how these urban worlds are constructed and how settings interact with characters and events.

Creative and Personal Writing

Shaun Tan's visual narratives inspire imaginative writing. A variety of types of creative writing activities could be used in secondary classrooms. For example, students could write short stories about a character who has just arrived in a strange new land. Another option is to reinterpret a section of a book as a poem, which encourages secondary students to connect and reflect (Seale 2015, 12). Creative writing could also be used as a form of assessment to demonstrate students' understanding of a text they read. For example, students could be asked to add a new chapter to *Tales from the Inner City* (Tan 2018) and write an author/artist statement explaining what they learned from previous chapters to be able to compose this new chapter. Alternatively, they could compose a song about a character's journey (e.g., using *Cicada* or *The Red Tree*). Griffith (2017) argues in favor of creative writing as an assessment, as student writing "adds some autonomy to reading, since rather than answering the same literary analysis questions across the board, students can individualize and personalize their work" (60).

Personal writing prompts should be used alongside the study of any of Tan's books to provide students with time and space to go deeper with Tan's texts without the pressure of composing a polished piece of writing. For example, students could be asked to reflect on the theme of belonging or consider how urban spaces are important to them. Students could then share this writing in classroom community "read-arounds" (Christensen 2017, 15). Shaun Tan's visual narratives give readers a lot to think about, so having frequent opportunities to stop and write can help students unpack these complex worlds.

Resonant Urban Landscapes

Shaun Tan's visual narratives contain urban landscapes that resonate deeply with readers. This artist and storyteller has produced such a varied body of work that teachers have a wide range of choice among the types of cities presented, the formats of these stories (e.g., picturebook, collection of tales, wordless book), and the possibilities for using these books in the classroom. Tan's works, with their powerful language and visuals, are necessary in today's classrooms because they invite careful observation, critical examination, and rich conversation. His visions of the city can be used to challenge and expand secondary students' understandings and invite them to enter into conversations about their own cities.

Things to Think About

1. After students learn about visual analysis concepts and apply them to Shaun Tan's books, they could illustrate a city from a novel they have read. What design choices do students make and what are the effects of those choices?
2. After exploring some of the stories in *Tales from the Inner City,* students could imagine their own versions of animals interacting with urban spaces and norms. What do these juxtapositions of the natural world and the urban world communicate to readers?
3. With the exception of the Fox chapter (page 188) in *Tales from the Inner City,* all the stories in this volume are told from the point of view of humans. What do students notice when they consider a story from the point of view of an animal?

Things to Explore

1. Shaun Tan's Website: http://www.shauntan.net
2. Fan-made video of *The Red Tree*: https://www.youtube.com/watch?v=PrmMFFpKxgw
3. Columbia Film Language Glossary: https://filmglossary.ccnmtl.columbia.edu
4. Urban Fishing Cat Conservation Project: https://fishingcats.lk/

Notes

1. *The Red Tree, The Lost Thing,* and *The Rabbits* are published in the volume *Lost and Found* (Tan 2011b).
2. "Picturebook" is intentionally written as one word throughout this chapter. As Hintz and Tribunella (2013) write, "Maria Nikolajeva and Carole Scott established that 'picturebook' should be spelled as one word . . . in order to signify that text and image are combined into a unified form" (160).

References

Bakis, Maureen. 2012. *The Graphic Novel Classroom: Powerful Teaching and Learning with Images.* Thousand Oaks, CA: Corwin.

Bang, Molly. 2016. *Picture This: How Pictures Work.* Rev. and expanded 25th anniversary ed. San Francisco: Chronicle.

Chappell, Bill. 2019."Chance the Snapper Is Snared: Alligator Caught after a Wild Week in Chicago Park." NPR, July 16. https://www.npr.org/2019/07/16/742215100/chance-the-snapper-is-snared-alligator-caught-after-a-wild-week-in-chicago-park.

Christensen, Linda. 2017. *Reading, Writing, and Rising Up: Teaching about Social Justice and the Power of the Written Word.* 2nd ed. Milwaukee, WI: Rethinking Schools.

Dallacqua, Ashley A., Sarah Kersten Parrish, and Minidi Rhoades. 2015. "Using Shaun Tan's Work to Foster Multiliteracies in 21st-Century Classrooms." *The Reading Teacher* 69(2): 207–17.

Davidson, Rjurik. 2010. "Painting a Motion Picture: An Interview with Shaun Tan." *Metro Magazine,* no. 166, 36–41.

Eisner, Will. 2008. *Graphic Storytelling and Visual Narrative.* New York: W.W. Norton & Company.

Griffith, Jason. 2017 *From Me to We: Using Narrative Nonfiction to Broaden Student Perspectives.* New York: Routledge.

Hintz, Carrie, and Eric L. Tribunella. 2013. *Reading Children's Literature: A Critical Introduction.* New York: Bedford/St. Martin's.

McCloud, Scott. 1993. *Understanding Comics: The Invisible Art.* New York: HarperCollins

The New London Group. 1996. "A Pedagogy of Multiliteracies: Designing Social Futures." *Harvard Educational Review* 66(1): 60–92.

Reid, Stephanie, and Michelle Dyer. 2018. "Brian Selznick's *Marvel*-ous Multimodal Novel: Exploring Images and Words with Eighth Grade English Students." *Voices from the Middle* 26(2): 53–58.

Rhoades, Mindi, Ashley Dallacqua, Sara Kersten, Johnny Merry, and Mary Catherine Miller. 2015. "The Pen(cil) is Mightier Than the (S)Word? Telling Sophisticated Silent Stories Using Shaun Tan's Wordless Graphic Novel, *The Arrival*." *Studies in Art Education* 56(4): 307–26.

Ruhemann, Andrew, and Shaun Tan, dirs. 2010. *The Lost Thing*. Victoria, Australia: Highly Spirited.

Seale, Tara. 2015. "Why Teach Poetry?" *English Journal* 104(4): 12–14.

Serafini, Frank. 2014. *Reading the Visual: An Introduction to Teaching Multimodal Literacy*. New York: Teachers College Press.

"Shaun Tan Interview: Tan on the Ellis Island Experience and His Illustrations in *The Arrival*." N.d. Scholastic. https://www.scholastic.com/teachers/videos/teaching-content/shaun-tan-interview-tan-ellis-island-experience-and-his-illustrations-arrival/

Stanton, Andrew, dir. 2008. *Wall-E*. Emeryville, CA: Pixar.

Tan, Shaun. 2001a. "Originality and Creativity." Joint National Conference of the Australian Association for the Teaching of English and the Australian Literacy Educators' Association, July 12–15, Hobart, Tasmania, Australia.

Tan, Shaun. 2001b. "Picture Books: Who Are They For?" Joint National Conference of the Australia Association for the Teaching of English and the Australian Literacy Educators' Association, July 12–15, Hobart, Tasmania, Australia.

Tan, Shaun. 2006. *The Arrival*. New York: Arthur A. Levine.

Tan, Shaun. 2008. *Tales from Outer Suburbia*. New York: Arthur A. Levine.

Tan, Shaun. 2010. *The Bird King: An Artist's Notebook*. New York Arthur A. Levine.

Tan, Shaun. 2011a. "The Accidental Graphic Novelist." *Bookbird: A Journal of International Children's Literature* 49(4): 1–9.

Tan, Shaun. 2011b. *Lost and Found*. New York: Arthur A. Levine.

Tan, Shaun. 2014. *Rules of Summer*. New York: Arthur A. Levine.

Tan, Shaun. 2015. *The Singing Bones*. New York: Arthur A. Levine.

Tan, Shaun. 2016. "Hooked (and a Bit Unsettled)." In *The Book That Made Me*, edited by Judith Ridge, 33–74. Somerville, MA: Candlewick Press.

Tan, Shaun. 2018. *Tales from the Inner City*. New York: Arthur A. Levine.

Tan, Shaun. 2019. *Cicada*. New York: Arthur A. Levine.

Vasudevan, Lalitha. 2010. "Research Directions: Literacies in a Participatory, Multimodal World: The Arts and Aesthetics of Web 2.0." *Language Arts* 88(1): 43–50.

Williams, Wendy, and James Blasingame. 2017. "Celebrating All Voices: Assuring Diversity in Young Adult Literature." In *Teaching Young Adult Literature Today: Insights, Considerations, and Perspectives for the Classroom Teacher*, 2nd ed., edited by Judith A. Hayn, Jeffrey S. Kaplan, and Karina R. Clemmons, 223–50. Lanham, MD: Rowman & Littlefield.

Editor Bios

Laura M. Nicosia, PhD, earned her doctorate at New York University and is Professor of English at Montclair State University, New Jersey, where she teaches all things American literature, young adult/children's literature, and literary theory. She is a New Jersey Council for the Humanities Public Scholar, serves as the New Jersey State Ambassador to the Assembly on Literature of Adolescents, and is Past-President of the New Jersey Council of Teachers of English. Nicosia is the author of *Educators Online: Preparing Today's Educators for Tomorrow's Digital Literacies* (Peter Lang, 2013), co-editor of *Through a Distorted Lens: Media as Curricula and Pedagogy in the 21st Century* (Sense, 2017), co-editor of *Critical Insights: John Steinbeck's* The Pearl (Salem/Grey House Press, 2019), and co-editor of *Notable American Women Writers,* volumes 1 and 2 (Salem/Grey House, 2020).

James F. Nicosia, PhD, earned his doctorate at New York University and is a writer, scholar, educational consultant, and children's literacy advocate. He served on the Voice of Youth Advocates Nonfiction Award Committee for the past two years and publishes the Boy Book of the Month website for reluctant readers (BoyBookoftheMonth.com). He is the author of *Reading Mark Strand: His Collected Works, Career, and the Poetics of the Privative* (Palgrave-Macmillan, 2008) and the co-editor of *Critical Insights: John Steinbeck's* The Pearl (Salem/Grey House, 2019) and *Notable American Women Writers,* volumes 1 and 2 (Salem/Grey House, 2020). His essays have appeared in such diverse publications as *Bloom's Major Poets* series, *Southern Studies,* and *Revista de Estudios Hispanicos.* He teaches Grammars of English, Young Adult Literature, and all periods of American literature at Montclair State University in New Jersey.

Contributor Bios

MARIA ANDREU is the author of *Love in English* (Balzer + Bray, 2021) and *The Secret Side of Empty* (Running Press Teens, 2014). Her work has appeared in *Teen Vogue*, *Newsweek*, *The Washington Post*, and *The Star-Ledger* (Newark, NJ). *The Secret Side of Empty* is a Junior Library Guild Selection, a National Indie Excellence Book Award winner, and an International Latino Book Awards Finalist. It has been called "captivating" by *School Library Journal*. Maria lives in New Jersey. Learn more about her work at MariaEAndreu.com.

KRISTINA D. BYBEE is a doctoral student in the English Education PhD program at Arizona State University. Her current research interests include independent reading strategies and multimodal communication. She is currently teaching first-year composition at Chandler-Gilbert Community College, and she taught English Language Arts in grades 8 through 12 in Arizona for sixteen years.

E.E. CHARLTON-TRUJILLO – Deemed a "force of nature" by *Kirkus Reviews*, Mexican American author, filmmaker, and activist e.E. Charlton-Trujillo grew up in Mathis, Texas. She is the recipient of the Delacorte Dell Yearling Award, the Parents' Choice Silver Honor, and the National Council for the Social Studies Notable Book honor, for her first novel, *Prizefighter En Mi Casa* (Perfection Learning, 2007). *Fat Angie* (Candlewick Press, 2019) garnered the American Library Association's Stonewall Award, was a Lambda Literary Finalist, and a Choose-to-Read Ohio book. *Fat Angie* was the catalyst for the documentary *At-Risk Summer*. The movie features stories from youth, educators, and award-winning authors, and from that experience, Charlton-Trujillo co-founded Never Counted Out, a nonprofit to bridge the gap between at-risk youth and artists. *Fat Angie: Rebel Girl Revolution* was released in 2019, and her picture book, *Lupe Lopez: Rock Star Rules*, co-written with *New York Times* best-selling author Pat Zietlow Miller and illustrated by Joe Cepeda, was published in 2020. Her varied projects can be found at bigdreamswrite.com.

Karen Coats – Having retired from Illinois State University, Karen Coats is now Professor of Education and Director of the Centre for Research in Children's Literature at Cambridge. She has also taught English Language Arts at the junior high and high school levels. Her most recent books include *The Bloomsbury Introduction to Children's and Young Adult Literature* (Bloomsbury Academic, 2018) and the co-edited volume *Teaching Young Adult Literature* (with Mike Cadden and Roberta Seelinger Trites, 2020) for the Modern Language Association's Options for Teaching Series.

Sean P. Connors is Associate Professor of English Education at the University of Arkansas. His scholarship and teaching focus on the application of diverse critical perspectives to young adult literature. He is the editor of *The Politics of Panem: Challenging Genres* (Sense Publishers, 2014), a collection of critical essays about the Hunger Games series, and co-editor of *Teaching Girls on Fire: Essays on Dystopian Young Adult Literature in the Classroom* (McFarland, 2020). Connors is the host of *The Storyteller's Thread*, a monthly podcast devoted to children's and young adult literature.

Mary Rand Hess is a poet, playwright, screenwriter, mixed-media artist, and *New York Times* best-selling author of notable and award-winning books such as *Solo* and *Swing* (Blink YA), co-authored with Newbery Medalist Kwame Alexander; *Animal Ark: Celebrating Our Wild World in Poetry and Pictures* (National Geographic Children's Books, 2017), co-authored with Alexander and Deanna Nikaido; *Photo Ark: Limited Earth Day Edition* (National Geographic Children's Books, 2020); *Little Larry Goes to School* (National Geographic Children's Books, 2019), written with renowned photographer and filmmaker, Gerry Ellis; *The One and Only Wolfgang: From Pet Rescue to One Big Happy Family* (Zonderkidz, 2019), co-authored with Steve Greig of @wolfgang2242 Instagram fame; and her forthcoming picture book *Belong* (Houghton Mifflin Harcourt). Mary loves collaboration and is currently at work on a few exciting projects, including a screenplay and a musical, which is scheduled to premiere at The Kennedy Center in 2021.

Melinda Knight is Professor of English and Founding Director of the Center for Writing Excellence at Montclair State University. Her research interests include the intersections of class, gender, identity, and race in American literature; manifestations of aestheticism and decadence; the impact of urbanization on cultural products; and representations of the American West. She earned a PhD in American civilization at New York University and a BA in Spanish and American literature at Cornell University.

Tricia M. Kress is Associate Professor in the Educational Leadership for Diverse Learning Communities EdD program at Molloy College in Rockville Centre, New York. Her research uses critical pedagogy, cultural sociology, and auto/ethnography to rethink teaching, learning, and research in urban schools in the United States. She is co-editor of the book series *Imagination and Praxis: Criticality and Creativity in Education and Educational Research* with Brill/Sense Publishers and *Transformative Imaginings: Critical Visions for the Past-Present-Future of Education* with DIO Press. Her co-edited volume *Paulo Freire's Intellectual Roots: Toward Historicity in Praxis* (edited with Robert Lake) received the Society of Professors of Education Book Award in 2014.

Angel Daniel Matos is Assistant Professor of Gender, Sexuality, and Women's Studies at Bowdoin College, specializing in youth literature, queer studies, and screen cultures. He frequently teaches courses on young adult literature, teen cinema, queer literature and media, and Latinx literature/culture. His work has been published in journals such as *Children's Literature, Research on Diversity in Youth Literature, The ALAN Review, QED: A Journal of GLBTQ Worldmaking,* and *Queer Studies in Media and Popular Culture,* in addition to a handful of edited volumes. He is one of the co-editors of *Media Crossroads: Intersections of Space and Identity in Screen Cultures,* which will be published in spring 2021 by Duke University Press. His monograph, tentatively titled *The Reparative Possibilities of Queer Young Adult Literature and Culture* (Routledge), is expected to be published in fall 2021.

Emma K. McNamara is Adjunct Professor of Education at the University of the District of Columbia in Washington, D.C. She has master's degrees in English education and children's literature from the University of the District of Columbia and Simmons College, respectively, and is dually certified in Culturally Responsive Literature Instruction from Harvard Graduate School of

Education. Her research interests include canon versus syllabus construction, bildungsroman, affective stylistics, and reading choice. She is an active member of the Children's Literature Association and the American Libraries Association, where she is the Recording Secretary for the Coretta Scott King Book Awards Executive Board and a member of the 2021 Margaret A. Edwards Award committee. She is slated to begin her PhD at Ohio State University in the fall of 2020.

Patricia Patrissy has been an educator for more than fifteen years. She received her MS in secondary education from the College of Staten Island, and her MS in information and library science from Pratt Institute. Currently she is a high school librarian at Fort Hamilton High School in Brooklyn, New York.

Benjamin Alire Sáenz is an author of poetry and prose for adults and teens. He is the winner of the PEN/Faulkner Award and the American Book Award for his books for adults. *Aristotle and Dante Discover the Secrets of the Universe* (Simon and Schuster, 2012) was a Printz Honor Book, the Stonewall Award winner, the Pura Belpre Award winner, the Lambda Literary Award winner, and a finalist for the Amelia Elizabeth Walden Award. His first novel for teens, *Sammy and Juliana in Hollywood* (Cinco Puntos Press, 2004), was an American Library Association Top Ten Book for Young Adults and a finalist for the Los Angeles Times Book Prize. His second book for teens, *He Forgot to Say Goodbye* (Simon and Schuster, 2008), won the Tomás Rivera Mexican American Children's Book Award, and the Southwest Book Award. His books have been translated worldwide.

Katie Sluiter is an eighth-grade English Language Arts (ELA) teacher in the Wyoming Public School District in Wyoming, Michigan, where she has taught middle and high school students for more than seventeen years. She is also a graduate student in the English education doctoral program at Western Michigan University. Katie has published and presented on the significant impact of young adult literature in the secondary classroom and the best practices of integrating it into an ELA curriculum. Areas she is interested in researching include multiage community-based reading programs and opportunities, the influence of author visits on student engagement and learning, and the methods of incorporating traditionally controversial topics with young adult literature in a middle-grade ELA classroom. She lives and reads with her family in Zeeland, Michigan.

WENDY R. WILLIAMS is Assistant Professor of English in the Interdisciplinary Humanities and Communication Department at Arizona State University (ASU). She studies visual narratives, multimodal writing, and out-of-school learning. She is the author of *Listen to the Poet: Writing, Performance, and Community in Youth Spoken Word Poetry* (University of Massachusetts Press, 2018) and is currently working on her next two books, *Mentoring Youth Writers* and *Visual Storytellers*. Her work has appeared in the *Journal of Adolescent and Adult Literacy*, the *Journal of Visual Literacy*, the *English Journal, Pedagogies: An International Journal, Teaching Young Adult Literature Today*, and elsewhere. Dr. Williams is the founding director of ASU's Young Authors' Studio, a free program for youth writers (grades 5–12) administered by college students. In addition, she teaches courses on narrative research methods, children's literature, young adult literature, visual narratives, and Studio Ghibli films.

Index